PISCATAQUA PAPERS

*Gardening from the Merrimack
to the Kennebec*

Published by the Piscataqua Garden Club
York Harbor, Maine

Postpaid Mail Order: "Piscataqua Papers"
P. O. Box 323
York Harbor, Maine

Thomas Todd Company
14 Beacon St., Boston, Mass.

Printed in the United States of America

Acknowledgements

The area from the Merrimack to the Kennebec, extending inland for about twenty-five miles, presents very special gardening problems for both the summer visitor and the year-round resident. The Piscataqua Garden Club, York Harbor, Maine, a member of the Garden Club of America, is publishing this handbook in hopes that it will be a helpful guide for gardeners, and interesting reading for anyone interested in this beautiful and historic part of the world.

We wish to extend our thanks to the outstanding guest writers who so generously contributed their expert talents to this book: William Howells, Professor of Anthropology at Harvard University; Henry Cadwalader, teacher of American History; Ernest Colprit, author, hybridist, of Colprit's Nursery, Dover, N. H., which has a most comprehensive collection of evergreens; the late E. Raymond Childs, rosarian; Cynthia Westcott, Ph.D. in plant pathology, internationally known plant doctor and rosarian; Professor Radcliffe B. Pike, Horticulture Section, Plant Science Department, University of New Hampshire; Betty Jane Hayward, a Vice President of the American Rock Garden Society, Fellow of the Royal Horticultural Society, lecturer and landscape designer; William Augustus Peirce, specialist in alpine plants; E. J. Rasmussen, Professor Emeritus of Horticulture, University of New Hampshire; Roland E. Roberts, Extension vegetable agent for the Department of Plant and Soil Sciences at the University of Maine, planner and executor of educational programs in both commercial vegetable production and home gardening; Edna Roberts, widely known grower of Gold Medal African Violets, other greenhouse plants and unusual annuals, owner of Cider Hill Greenhouses, York, Maine; Olin Sewall Pettingill, Jr., Ph.D., Director Cornell University Laboratory of Ornithology and editor of *Enjoying Maine Birds*; Christopher Packard, Director, Maine Audubon Society and Portland Society of Natural History, Publisher of *Enjoying Maine Birds*; Dorothy Hinitt, editor of the *Bulletin* of the Garden Club of America, for permission to reprint several articles which appeared in that publication.

Guest authors are further identified by their addresses, which appear with their names at the head of their articles. All other writers are members of the Piscataqua Garden Club.

I would particularly like to thank all the members of the Piscataqua Garden Club who have contributed their literary talents and financial aid, and other friends who have been so generous with their advice and time. Special thanks must go to Elizabeth C. Neilson for the cover design and general book design, and to Anne Peirce for additional art work, and to my fellow editors, SARAH R. CHILDS, BARBARA CHENEY, MARION P. HOSMER, and HARRIET ROBESON, for their hard work and boundless enthusiasm.

CAROLINE CADWALADER
York Harbor, Maine

❧

Sponsors

Mrs. Clifton McC. Bockstoce	Mrs. Alfred R. McIntyre
Mrs. Henry Cadwalader	Mrs. Marshall S. Morgan
Miss Barbara Cheney	Mrs. Alexander S. Neilson
Mrs. E. Raymond Childs	Mrs. William G. Northrup
Mrs. George Coggill	Mrs. Jefferson Patterson
Mrs. John Cutter	Mrs. Herman Pike
Mrs. John Emerson	Mrs. Fergus Reid, Jr.
Mrs. Allyn B. Forbes	Mrs. Harold G. Richard
Mrs. Henry Fuller	Mrs. Urbain Robert
Mrs. Joe W. Gerrity	Miss Harriet A. Robeson
Mrs. Edward Greene, Jr.	Mrs. Sherwood Rollins
Mrs. Lucien Horton	Mrs. Dudley S. Stark
Mrs. Calvin Hosmer, Jr.	Mrs. Alexander B. Warrick
Mrs. Nils R. Johaneson	Mrs. Valentine Wood

Table of Contents

History and Early Gardens

Early Peoples

William Howells,
Kittery Point, Me.

THE first people to see the Piscataqua River were not gardeners. They were hunters, probably looking for mammoth, filtering eastward from the Great Plains and the lake region, about 9,000 B.C., when Kittery and York were tundra. At any rate, such hunters left a collection of mammoth-spear points at Ipswich, where they had a large camp site, and traces of them have now been found in Nova Scotia as well.

As the glacier melted northward, later hunters and fishers settled in, making new kinds of javelin points, using nets for fishing on the shore, and eating clams and oysters so prodigiously that they left big shell heaps along the coast of Maine. Here they have become popularly known as the Red Paint people, because of spreading red ocher in the graves of the dead. Some of these Indians built a very large wier to trap fish in the tidewaters of the Charles, roughly along Berkeley and Boylston streets in Boston's Back Bay. This was about 4,000 B.C. Only very late did the use of plants come into New England from the south, and not at first in a form which would have watered a Pilgrim's mouth — the Eastern Indians began with such things as sunflower and ragweed seeds, with gourds and pumpkins coming afterwards. By about 700 B.C. corn had made the long trip from Mexico to New York, and can only have reached the Northeast later still.

It seems likely, to archaeologists and students of Indian languages, that those later hunters were already speaking Algonkian languages, i.e., that this family had become distinct from the originally related Muskoghean languages of the south by about 2,500 B.C. at the latest. There were well-defined divisions of Algonkian-speakers when the Europeans arrived. The Abenakis of Maine, like the Micmacs beyond them, were still primarily hunters, though they were growing corn in a half-hearted way as well. Their neighbors in southern New Hampshire, the Penacooks, were more settled agriculturalists, living in low huts covered with bark or mats, and making pottery in a style they had learned from the Iroquois to the west. The first white to come here found two Penacook tribes close to the sea: the Pascataqua, near Dover, New Hampshire, and the Agamenticus across the river, the only Penacooks in Maine.

It would be nice, remembering the first Thanksgiving in Massachusetts, to imagine the settlers and the Indians sitting on Strawbery Banke to discuss strawberries, or even arrange a flower or so. But these first meetings are totally unrecorded, and there were probably no Indians actually living

3

at Portsmouth, nor any significant contact there. (A Phillip Swaddow, evidently a squatter, had a "wigwam" in the 1630's where Alexander Shapleigh shortly built his house in Kittery Point — what does that mean?) The English, of course, arrived with full title, from the Plymouth Company, to the whole coast, Indians or no Indians. And they immediately gave the Penacooks smallpox, drastically reducing their numbers. All this simplified problems of settlement from the settlers' point of view. Nevertheless the Indians and the English had generally friendly relations, although resistance by the former, which reached expression in occasional massacres, as at Eliot and Durham, long kept the settlers from penetrating to the White Mountains. Eventually, however, the latter bought up all the land, in good legal fashion which the Indians did not comprehend, and drove the last organized remnants of the Penacooks into Canada.

Reference:
Ancient Man in North America, by H. M. Wormington

Exploration and Colonial History

Roberta Horton and Henry Cadwalader,
York Harbor, Me.

THE history of the early exploration of the Northeastern Coast of New England can never be written with accuracy since the hardy mariners from the west coast of England, the French Channel ports, Portugal and the Basque ports of Spain left no written records of their early voyages to this part of the world. There is no question, however, that for at least 50 years prior to 1600 the coast of Maine was well known to European sailors and fishermen to whom the enormous quantities of fish off the New England coast were a chief source of livelihood. The name 'Maine' itself is a reminder that for a long time the use of islands, such as the Isles of Shoals, for drying fish, was of primary concern, antedating the colonization of the 'Main' land, which was to come later. Fish at this period were an essential item of diet, not only in Roman Catholic France and Spain, but also on Church of England fast days, whose number was increased by Queen Elizabeth in order to build up the fishing fleet as a school for mariners. All early accounts of voyages to the New World tell of the marvelous numbers of fish to be seen, even on the ocean surface. As late as 1794 Moreau de St. Mery wrote, "A little after sunrise a tremendous sea came out of the southwest, though the wind did not blow at all from that direction, and continued for more than an hour, bringing with it myriads of all sorts of fish, some of them six feet long. They

4

seemed distressed and almost carried away by the sea, which was, so to speak, alive with them and at the same time solidified by them. When the ship plunged between two waves, the fish on each side threatened to overwhelm us; and when a wave subsided, the fish, over an area of many yards, were left without water and slid nosily over one another. What a prodigious spectacle! Never will it be erased from my memory!"

Recorded history begins with John Cabot's voyage in 1498, followed by a series of European explorers who visited the Maine coast during the 16th century. Finally in 1602 Captain Bartholomew Gosnold paid a noteworthy visit to the York area which is the center of the region of our interest. Landing on Cape Neddick near the Nubble, he encountered a group of natives who spoke 'divers Christian words' and whose leader was dressed in European clothes. In 1605 another English explorer, George Weymouth, sailed along the Maine coast and captured five Indians whom he took back to England. Three of these lived in the household of Sir Ferdinando Gorges who thus learned about Maine and became the leader in its colonization.

Widespread interest now having been aroused in England in the possibilities of profits to be won in American colonization, the London and Plymouth companies were incorporated by King James in 1606, Gorges being an enthusiastic member of the latter group. The first attempted colony in Maine was sent out in 1607 but survived only one year at the mouth of the Kennebec. In 1609 French Jesuits established a permanent mission on Mt. Desert Island. By now hundreds of ships were making regular trips to the Maine coast for fishing and trading, headquarters for which enterprises being established at Monhegan.

In 1614 Captain John Smith made his famous exploration of the North American Coast, and after this his lectures and the map which he published fired anew the interest of Englishmen, including Prince Charles who gave the area the name 'New England.'

The early failure to establish permanent colonies on the Maine coast was partly due to a belief that Englishmen could not endure its rugged climate. Sir Ferdinando Gorges accordingly organized an expedition headed by Dr. Richard Vines for the express purpose of learning how to survive a New England winter. This group wintered at the mouth of the Saco River during the season of 1616-17 and ministered to the natives during the terrible plague which that year killed 9 out of every 10 Indians from Maine to the Hudson River.

In 1620 the Council for New England, the successor to the Plymouth Company, obtained a grant of the country between 40° and 48° North Latitude and in 1622 Gorges and John Mason received from the Council a grant of 'The Province of Maine' extending from the Merrimack to the Kennebec Rivers. In 1629 they divided this up, Gorges taking the area from the Piscataqua north to the Kennebec, while Mason retained the area which is now roughly New Hampshire.

From all this it can be seen that there is no justification for the traditional viewpoint that New England settlement began with the Pilgrims and Puritans. In fact it was the report of Dr. Vines' successful winter at the mouth of Saco which encouraged the Pilgrims to make their venture to the New World. It was also thanks to the friendly help and advice of Tisquantum, one of the three Abenaki Indians who had lived for a time in England with Sir Ferdinando Gorges, that the Plymouth Colonists were able to survive the first winter in Massachusetts.

By 1630 when the first of the tremendous migration of Puritans reached the area around Boston they were greeted by Sir Ferdinando's associates and relatives who had already settled there. These latter Church of England people, loyal to the Crown, were soon dismayed by the stiff-necked and hostile attitude of the newcomers and so turned their attention to resettlement in a more friendly atmosphere in New Hampshire and Maine.

Beween 1623 and 1631 settlements were established along the New England coast from Little Harbor and Strawbery Banke on the Piscataqua to Casco Bay. Agamenticus, now York, was founded about 1630 by Colonel Walter Norton, one of the dissatisfied Massachusetts settlers, and Edward Godfrey, who had been sent out by Gorges to take charge of a fishing enterprise established at what is now Newcastle, New Hampshire. Godfrey was fascinated by the possibilities of the harbor and the fertile soil at Agamenticus and having built himself a house there communicated his enthusiasm to Norton. Norton and Godfrey obtained a charter in 1631 from Gorges for the Agamenticus plantation, so called from the Indian name for the river which forms the harbor. Mt. Agamenticus was then called by the Abenaki Indians 'Sasanoa's Mount,' after one of their great Chiefs.

It is thus apparent that the people who settled New Hampshire and Maine were very different from the dissenters and separatists of Massachusetts. The former were supporters of the Crown and the established church and intended as far as possible to reproduce in America the kind of life they had left behind in England.

In 1641, Agamenticus having grown in size and importance, Sir Ferdinando drew up a charter and changed its name to Gorgeana in his own honor.

From this time on preoccupation with the civil war in England resulted in affairs in America being allowed to run their own course. As the power of the Puritan party increased, so did the desire of the Massachusetts Bay colonists to take over the rich plantations to the east. In 1652 the Province of Maine was annexed to Massachusetts and the name of Gorgeana was changed to York. Following the restoration of Charles II, Gorges' grandson reacquired title to his grandfather's estate but quickly sold it back to agents of the Massachusetts Colony. As everyone knows, Maine finally became independent once more in 1820 under one of the provisions of the famous Missouri Compromise.

It is probable that the people of Maine fared better under the protection of the powerful Massachusetts government than they would have on their own. From the outbreak of King Philip's War in 1675 to the end of the French and Indian War in 1763 the English inhabitants of New England were in constant fear of attack by hostile Indians. In spite of Massachusetts troops stationed in Portsmouth, the massacre and capture of about 150 residents of York in January 1692 was one of the most frightful tragedies of the colonial period. On the brighter side, Sir William Phipps, Governor of the Province of Maine, had, in 1690, led a successful attack on the French settlement of Port Royal in Nova Scotia. Again in 1745 another Maine man, Sir William Pepperrell, commanded a New England expedition which captured the French fortress at Louisburg.

From 1763, the close of the French and Indian War, to the outbreak of the Revolution, the people of Maine for the most part sided with the other colonies in their opposition to the new pressures applied by the Royal Government. York had its version of the famous Boston Tea Party, as did most of the ports on the Atlantic Coast.

Those who would like to pursue this fascinating study further are directed to the bibliography which follows. Although the latter two books are out of print, they are available in local libraries.

Bibliography:

ERNST, George, *New England Miniature, A History of York, Maine.* Freeport, Maine. The Bond Wheelwright & Co., 1961.

BANKS, Charles E., *History of York, Maine,* 2 Vols. Boston, The Calkins Press, 1931 and 1935.

MOODY, Edward C., *Agamenticus, Gorgeana, York.* Augusta, Me. Press of the Kennebec Journal Company for the York Publishing Co., 1914.

Colonial Compromise

Sarah R. Childs

THIS is one horticulturalist's compromise with the antiquarians. I presume it will be more popular with the horticulturalists than with the antiquarians.

I have, for the past eight years, been Garden Chairman of the Society of Colonial Dames in the State of New Hampshire, who maintain The Moffat-Ladd House in Portsmouth. The house was built in 1762 and the gardens cover nearly two acres.

At first, it was just a delightful horticultural operation. Then we started hearing the words 'Museum Houses' and 'Museum Gardens' and it all became a different problem. Of necessity, I have acquired some knowledge of Colonial Gardens and more of how to compromise.

The reason for compromise is that, as an horticulturalist, I cannot bring myself to use inferior plant material just to be traditional. A great many of the 17th and 18th century plants are beautiful, and still used and loved by us today. There has been no need to improve them. Others, due to the work of the plant breeders, have been changed and are much better. The twentieth century hybrids of these are more compact, robust, and disease resistant, have larger blossoms, a longer flowering season, and come in much more pleasing colors. Could it be that the Garden of Eden was mostly magenta?

There are certain plants that fulfill definite requirements in our gardens. All of these may not be on the lists of Colonial Flowers. However, to rationalize — certainly many plants from foreign countries were brought home by travellers and used in their individual gardens, if not generally. This gives us a slight — if questionable — justification for using them. But, if we need them, should we have to substitute with something less desirable?

I, personally, feel that we should try to reproduce the atmosphere and feeling of the eighteenth century garden without confining ourselves to ALL its limitations. Obviously, this could be a very controversial statement.

I believe that the design of a garden, its background, its accessories, and the arrangement of its planting is more important in creating an atmosphere than is its actual plant material.

In the Colonial Gardens, most of these factors were the result of both necessity and heredity.

The fact that practically every garden was enclosed was certainly primarily due to necessity! It was to keep the animals out. First, especially in New England, we had the 'front door' gardens. These were usually fenced in with wood, were quite small, and, always, contained the most precious plants. They were safe from chickens, cows, and horses.

Then, when life became easier and more gracious, there were the formal gardens, usually at the back of the house. They were enclosed by brick or stone walls, hedges, snake fences, or more elaborate painted ones which were sometimes combined with brick. Although these walls or hedges gave the added boon of privacy, they were primarily to shut out the uncultivated land and, again, the animals.

Every garden, small or large, had herbs. This was definitely a necessity. It provided medicines for the family, as well as seasoning for their food.

There was frequently a place for vegetables within the enclosure, and,

8

also, for fruit trees. These trees were often espaliered and the art of grafting was well known and much used.

Heredity played an important part. Seeds were brought with the settlers from England, Holland, and France. These thrived when planted in the rich soil. Many native plants were used too, and the general effect was of crowded abundance. In addition to the seeds, the settlers brought with them the memories, plans, and traditions of their home gardens.

These gardens were largely formal and architectural in character. The plan was definitely geometric and symmetrical, giving a feeling of balanced straight lines. There were many paths — either of brick, marl, pebbles, or crushed oyster shells. The reason that the paths were never grassed was that the lawn-mower was not invented until 1868. Orchards were mowed with scythes, but grass paths could not be kept neatly trimmed.

The service walks were practical and direct but the paths in the garden made geometric designs. Knots and mazes were popular and, later on, there was an enthusiasm for parterres.

The beds were usually edged with borders of box, privet, hyssop, and sometimes germander.

Many garden accessories were used but practically no statuary. Ornamental bee-hives were very popular. Benches, arbors, trellises, and even dovecotes were common, and a sun-dial was considered a necessity. Fountains were used in the south — if at all.

If we keep or reproduce the plan of the Colonial Garden, make use of the accessories typical of the period, include herbs, attempt to achieve the same abundance of bloom, use as many of the old plants as possible, then, I think, we have created the feeling and atmosphere of a Colonial Garden. And if, in getting this effect we have profited by the great strides in plant breeding that have been made in the past three hundred years — is it not a satisfactory compromise between the horticulturalist and the antiquarian? I believe it is. Even museum houses have compromised to the extent of installing modern plumbing.

Colonial Gardens

Ruth D. Mathes

FLOWERS and gardens have been a source of great joy to mankind since the world began. The Chinese have a wise saying which was found in a book of proverbs. "If you would be happy for a week, take a wife; if you would be happy for a month, kill your pig; but if you would be happy all your life, plant a garden."

As the Puritans neared this country John Winthrop wrote in his journal, "There came a smell off the shore like the smell of a garden." There is no doubt that every Puritan woman bore with her across the seas some little package of seeds and bulbs or a tiny slip or plant. Fifty years after the landing of the Pilgrims at Plymouth there were growing all manner of herbs and medicine, and gardens of flowers. In Colonial days shrewd and capable women of the colonies found the selling of flower seeds a congenial occupation. It must have been pleasant to buy packages of flower seeds at the same time and place where you bought your best bonnet and have all sent home in a bandbox together, and long after the bonnet was gone, the sweet peas and larkspur would recall its becoming charms.

The first nursery man in the new world was stern Governor Endicott of Salem. He said, "We find all thoughtful men of influence and prominence in all the colonies raising various fruits and selling trees and plants." In 1728 was established by John Bartram in Philadelphia the first botanical garden in America.

Throughout New England every home had its garden. The front yard garden was very popular. The New England houses were suited in color and outline to their front yards. Sarah Orne Jewett in her "A Mournful Villager" has drawn a beautiful picture of these front yard gardens. The front yard was not a garden of pleasure. Children could not play in those precious little enclosed plots and never could pick the flowers. Everyone who had enough social dignity to have a front door and a parlor also desired a front yard with flowers as an external token of that honored standing. Among flowers found there were: tiger lilies, larkspur, phlox, sweet William, lupine, poppies, Canterbury bells, violets, snapdragons and, often, an arbor of roses.

Then there were "The Side of the House" and "Back Door" gardens, with scarlet runners, portulacas, marigolds, nasturtiums, morning glories, hollyhocks, sweet geraniums, lemon verbena, ground pinks, tulips, peonies, sweet peas, flowering almond, lily of the valley and often — at any corner — would be found lilac and syringa bushes.

In more formal gardens boxwood was a favorite hedging. Bricks and boards were sometimes used to keep the flowers in place. Candytuft or sweet alyssum, as borders, set off well the many colored blooms of the garden. Sometimes ageratum was used as an edging. Quite formal were the sunken and water gardens. The water gardens were pretty with hyacinths, lilies and lotus leaves.

The herb gardens did not have the beauty and color of flowers, but how pleasant was that most pleasing odor! There were found all sorts of herbs: rosemary, rue, balm, anise, arnica, catnip, caraway, chives, camomile and dill being a few of them. The sowing, gathering and drying, and saving of these herbs was not simple. In the garret of every old house were hung bunches of herbs waiting for winter use. What a delightful fragrance that garret must have had!

Lilac, syringa and forsythia bushes must have a special mention. The universal flower in the old time garden was the lilac. Bushes shaded the front yard, were grown by the kitchen doorstep, sprung up beside the barn and shaded the well. Also lilac bushes were used to form hedges. In March the forsythia blooms were a delight to eyes and heart — a promise of spring — like golden sunshine.

Sundials were often placed in the gardens. Mottos or poems were engraved on the dials. On one which I know we found the following:

> "Time is too slow for those who wait,
> Too swift for those who fear,
> Too long for those who grieve,
> Too short for those who rejoice,
> But for those who love
> Time is Eternity."

My Grandmother's Garden on the Isles of Shoals

Rosamond Thaxter

MORE than three score years of brilliant sunshine and salt sea breezes have blown over the Isles since Celia Thaxter's garden bloomed in all its glory, the joy and wonder of those who beheld it. All the topsoil, painstakingly collected, enriched and planted by her loving hands has blown away. That blaze of bloom is no more, but perhaps there is one fat toad left to sun himself and tell a passing sea-gull of the Island Garden which Celia Thaxter, in her later years, planted and tended near her girlhood home, ten miles from the shore of New Hampshire and southern Maine.

When she was asked, "How do you make your plants flourish like this? What is your secret?" Celia Thaxter answered with one word: "Love — you may give them all they need of food and drink and make the conditions of their existence as favorable as possible. They may grow and bloom, but there is a certain ineffable something that will be missing if you do not love them, a delicate glory too spiritual to be caught and put into words! The Norwegians have a pretty and significant word, 'Opelske' which they use in speaking of the care of flowers. It means literally 'loving up' or cherishing them into health and vigor."

11

"Mine is just an old fashioned garden where flowers come together to praise the Lord and teach all who look upon them to do likewise," she writes in "An Island Garden" which is instructive reading today! She spared no small detail or suggestion which she felt might prove useful. Now there are modern short cuts to baking a cake, or doing the family laundry, but it still takes a seed the same time to develop into the joy of the full bloom flower! Celia said: "Each seed is a tiny casket in which lie folded roots, stalks, leaves, buds, flowers and seed vessels, surpassing in color, and beautiful form, all power of description." There were 57 different kinds of flowers in her little garden. Her favorites were wallflowers, violets, roses, lilies, sweet peas, mignonettes, heliotrope with a dash of honeysuckle all lavish of their scent which floated out on the pure sea air. Every blossom and plant seemed to have a more brilliant hue than elsewhere. The salt air and the peculiar richness of the soil gave a luxuriance of growth.

In early March she arrived at Appledore Island laden with boxes of seedlings which she had planted in her sunny Portsmouth windows. When the ground had been prepared and fertilized with good barn manure and the spring sun of April shone down warm on the slope running down to the sea, she transplanted each individual young shoot. Some of the frailest of these she had planted in egg shells, that the small roots might have added protection from strong winds and heavy rain. She had many disappointments as in any garden — a migration of sparrows might alight long enough to pull up every sweet pea from the ground, but their place was soon filled with Shirley poppies which became a symbol of "The Thaxter Parlor." Here music, painting, and poetry filled many unforgettable hours. There are a few fortunate persons who still remember rising early in the dewy morning, to join their white-haired friend at the wicket garden gate. There they watched fascinated as she snipped the hairy green stems and plunged them deep into a pitcher of water still warm from her bath. Thanks to this method the petals of the delicate poppies, just unfolded, did not loose their freshness, when arranged by the loving hands of the poet artist on the low book shelves. The pure white flowers were followed by those of a delicate pink which deepened into flame like the sunrise itself — an arrangement never to be forgotten by all those who saw it.

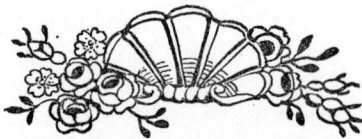

Practical Horticulture

Wind, Salt, and Gardens

Marion P. Hosmer

IT has never been unusual to find gardens near the sea, taking advantage of its coolness and moisture, adding their fragrance to the deliciousness of its salt breath, and softening with color of flowers and trees the wide stretches of its waters. For centuries, gardens on all the shores of the world have been described by their loving owners. Gardens large and small, simple and costly, on the Aegean, the Mediterranean, the Atlantic and the Pacific have given happiness and contentment to those who tended them. Many of the oldest and most historic gardens of this country are found on the New England coast, on land facing the open ocean, tucked away in snug harbors, or lying along sunny estuaries. Here on the southern edge of Maine we have no warm waters to make our winds gentle, as do the gardeners on Cape Cod or on the border of Long Island Sound; but neither must we contend with the scorching sun which burned the Greek and Roman gardens in the summer. Our worst enemies are wind and salt spray, and the wind must be regarded as an almost ever-present force — the gardener's fiercest opponent.

Before a seaside garden is located, the ways of the wind and as many of its vagaries as possible should be taken under consideration. To fight this strongest foe of plants are natural woods and slopes, buildings, walls of wood and stone, and planted windbreaks. It is interesting to notice while driving through the coastal towns, how wisely the oldest houses are placed to take advantage of the natural protection from wind and cold. The people who built them had no central heating to keep them snug through the New England winters on the edge of the sea, but a house facing south, and shielded by a wood or a land mass to the west and north-northeast, would trap the sun and be safe from the worst of the wind and snow.

Curiously enough, the most devastating wind here is not from the sea, but a wind that the farmers love to have for the haying — the strong, absolutely dry wind from the west, which blows hard for many of the days in each summer. The weather is always fair when the west wind blows, and the temperature may be fairly high. In an hour this wind, even when it blows cool, can draw every bit of moisture from the ground, and reduce a garden to a wilted, flattened state which is only relieved when the wind drops with the sun, and the discouraged gardener brings out the hose. Here, to the west, is where the defenses must be built high and strong; of wood or stone, or a thick wall of arbor vitae or spruce. Never plant hemlock or white pine for a windbreak near the sea as they will be badly

15

burned by the salt. An ideal orientation would be to face the garden a little east of south, and to build it as a feature of the house, a room out-of-doors. In this way the house itself could form one of the wind or salt breaks, and this plan also affords the seclusion which any well-planned garden should offer, and an opportunity for intimate knowledge of the garden's life. Many extra moments of pleasure and relaxation can be enjoyed, and small chores accomplished, because the garden is close by.

The best way to save a garden from salt spray is to place it out of the sea's reach, but since Maine has become a real part of the 'Hurricane Belt,' this has become more of a problem, and the salt has caused much serious damage. If the garden is small and near at hand, this can be lessened by washing off the spray with a forceful stream from the hose as soon as possible after the storm. Ordinary 'northeasters,' even a three-day one, do no more than batter the plants, and the trace minerals that the spray showers on the earth are known to be extremely valuable. After a recent hurricane which blackened the foliage of every apple tree, it was noticed during the following spring that the scab and sooty blotch infesting the old trees had almost entirely disappeared, and very little spraying had to be done that summer to get a fine crop of prime apples. Perhaps we should use diluted sea-water to spray our trees and plants, instead of the poison that can be so harmful. Salt from this same hurricane which so benefited the apple trees, completely killed the peach trees in the open orchard, but left unharmed one that was espaliered on the lee side of the house, which seems to indicate that it takes more than just salt-filled air to do permanent damage — the plants must be really deluged with sea-water.

One of the first pieces of advice given to me here was to have two garden areas, one for the morning and another for the afternoon. However warm a spring or summer morning is in the garden on the sea side, the wind almost inevitably comes off the water after lunch, bringing a chill that drives even the most ardent weeder to the other side of the house. Here can be the plants that don't need quite so much sun, and that are sensitive to salt; the broad-leaved evergreens and azaleas, most of the lilies, and the beautiful tuberous begonias that grow so luxuriantly in the cool moist air from the ocean.

To acknowledge the difficulties of a seaside garden is to have partly overcome them. To locate the garden in a spot sheltered from the fiercest blasts of the wind, as much as possible away from the salt spray, and to choose plants adapted by nature to its special conditions, is to be well started on the road to success.

The Breaking Waves Dash High

Ernest S. Colprit,
Dover, N. H.

THE State of Maine can boast of the most beautiful and varied coast-line in America. Its jutting headlands have to withstand the continuous onslaught of the sea. Salt spray is thrown high in the air at times and is borne far inland by the easterly gales. This does not seem like a very congenial climate for plants. However, nature has provided vegetation suitable for just such conditions. The rocky shore from Kittery to the Islands of Fundy is clothed with a variety of interesting and attractive plants which tenaciously cling to the almost soil-less ledges.

The highland cranberry (*Vaccinium vitis idaea minus*) is the most ven-turesome of all. A tiny shrub, its creeping stems are clothed with ever-green leaves and in the fall it bears myriads of bright red fruits much prized for sauce and jelly. Carpets of bunchberry (*Cornus canadensis*) are clothed with white flowers in spring and vivid with red berries in late summer and fall. The three leaved cinquefoil (*Potentilla tridentata*) is a shrubby plant six to eight inches high which spreads by underground stems and bears small white flowers in mid-summer. Bearberry (*Arc-tostaphylos uva arsi*) is also a widely trailing plant with evergreen leaves and cranberry-like red berries in the fall. *Campanula rotundifolia*, com-monly called " Blue Bells of Scotland" blooms all summer from its home in a crevice of the ledge. Colonies of these low-growing plants, when well established, make a charming ground cover about the seaside home.

Of the evergreens with needle-like foliage, the juniper stands salt spray best of all and carpets the brink of many a cliff and flourishes to the waterline of many a beach or cove. The common juniper (*Juniperus com-munis*) is quite variable. It may be found creeping over ledges to a depth of only a few inches or arching up to three or four feet when found further from the shore. Its foliage is bronzy green with silvery reflex. A more rare type is *Juniperus horizontalis* which creeps or trails about the rocks with charming effect. Cultivated clones of this species show only slight variations in habit but have foliage in different shades of blue or green. The Bar Harbor and Waukegan Junipers are popular varieties. Not so well known but equally as good are *J. planifolius*, *J. petraeus* and *J. pul-chellus*. The Chinese Junipers, *J. pfitzeriana* and *J. sargenti*, and their sub-varieties are also satisfactory at the shore.

Although this is the 'Pine Tree State' the native white pine does not stand salt spray and is found at its best in areas away from the shore or

17

protected from easterly winds. The Scotch and Austrian Pines are more amenable to bleak conditions but the picturesque Japanese Black Pine is best of all for very windy spots. For foundation planting the Mugho Pine is found to be quite satisfactory as is also the Japanese Yew in its spreading forms. Our native white cedar (*Thuya occidentalis*) or arbor vitae is found growing right down to the shoreline in swampy areas, so plenty of water should be applied to upland plantings. The red cedar (*Juniperus virginiana*) does well at the seashore but is liable to be windswept into fantastic shapes. Evergreen bittersweet (*Euonymus fortunei*), a broad-leaved evergreen, is quite resistant to salt spray and can be used in many spots about the home grounds as vine or groundcover but *Euonymus vegetus* can be used as an evergreen shrub about the house.

Many types of flowering shrubs are found near the shore and can be used to good advantage about the home. The red-fruited elder (*Sambucus pubens*) provides a beautiful display of creamy white flowers followed by brilliant red fruits in summer. It is much more restrained in its growth habit than the common black elder (*Sambucus canadensis*) which is also a desirable variety with its immense clusters of white flowers and black berries in the fall. The aronia or chokeberry is another good berry-bearing shrub. *Aronia melanocarpa* has black fruits and *A. arbutifolia* has bright red berries. The cultivated variety, *Aronia brilliantissima,* as its name indicates, is the most beautiful of all. Shad bush (*Amalanchier*) is found in several different forms and is readily transplanted. It is the earliest blooming of our shrubs with white or pinkish white flowers. Bayberry is found flourishing even on sand dunes but is difficult to transplant successfully unless dug with a large ball. The high bush cranberry (*Virburnum americanum*) is fine where a large shrub can be used. Its cranberry-like fruits are made into a jelly used by generations of "Down Easters" as a slightly pungent sauce with the meat course. *Virburnum lentago* bears a large blue fruit which is also considered edible.

While the wild roses (*Rosa nitida* and *R. virginiana*) are plentiful on the shore, it is a Japanese variety (*Rosa rugosa*) which has invaded the country and become one of the most beautiful of our seaside shrubs. The large pink or red blooms continue all summer and the large red rose-hips are showy in summer and fall. Various rugosa hybrids, such as Grootendorst with its rambler type clusters of double blooms on an erect shrub, are also successfully grown at the shore. A Canadian rose (*Therese Bugnet*) has semi-double wild rose pink blooms and is continuously in flower. Native honeysuckles (*Lonicera edulis* and *L. canadensis*) are to be found but it is the common garden honeysuckles (*L. tatarica* and *L. morrowi*) which have been widely seeded by the birds and contribute much to the landscape. The dwarf bush honeysuckle (*Diervilla lonicera*) is a common native spreading shrub with small yellow blooms in terminal spikes.

Southern bush honeysuckle (*Diervilla sessilifolia*) is more compact and much more ornamental.

The Russian olive (*Elaeagnus angustifolia*) has narrow silvery leaves and the small yellow blossoms are fragrant. At the seashore it becomes quite wind-swept and does not grow as tall as it does inland. The Korean variety (*Elaeagnus umbellatus*) grows into a large dense shrub with broad olive-green leaves. It bears quantities of waxy pink fruits which birds appreciate and in Korea these berries are used for sauce. A related plant, the buffalo berry (*Shepherdia argentea*) is a native of our western plains where its yellow or orange fruits were eaten by the Indians. It has narrow silvery leaves like the Russian olive but is also covered with sharp thorns. The flowers are not sexually perfect so they should not be planted singly.

Plantings of the shrubs we have mentioned will blend into the scenery without spoiling the natural beauty of the Maine coastal areas.

A Seaside Experience

Helen McIntyre

WHEN first I came to own a house in York after nearly twenty years of renting cottages, I thought, at last, a garden. Fortunately I found before I started that this was not feasible, but green surroundings seemed simple, so I plunged in, all ignorance, and planted things because they had the right effect against the house or because I liked them. They flourished for all too short a time. Then I began to find out what it was to live on rock ledge, with its shallow soil, at the bottom of a steep slope down which heavy rains wash like Niagaras; and as close to the ocean as one can be. The rhododendrons which looked so beautiful, filling in an awkward corner and concealing a straggle of ugly little windows, began to look sick and although a wire roof had been over them in winter from the first and a screen of burlap and pine branches provided to protect them from the burning wind of spring, they died a lingering death. Everyone prescribed, and I fussed over them as though they were orchids, but finally gave up and put in bush honeysuckles. These I had first rejected with scorn, as I don't much like them and there seemed to be so many of them everywhere. Now I know why. They grow. To be sure they get leggy, but if every other stalk is cut down to the ground in fall, the fresh growth fills in. Deciduous shrubs are really more sensible by the sea, for come an unusual storm, and there is one every so often, the evergreens tend to become never greens. I do have a few flourishing junipers well back from the house but close to, they would be a fire hazard.

In the little space between the house and the cliffs, bittersweet so flourished as to be almost menacing. But with a little training and constant snipping of the long tendrils, it has become a comfort. That long mound of green is very restful to the eye when the glitter of the water becomes a glare.

When I had planted a steep rocky bank with seven varieties of native ferns, guaranteed to grow in full sun, I was very pleased with the effect of the different textures and shades of green. Because of my shameful ignorance some hay scented fern was included. In two or three years I had a bank of hay scented fern with only a few other sturdy survivors still holding out on the high rocky spots. The mistake is mortifying but the hay scented fern stays beautifully green into October when some other kinds have turned brown, and the fragrance at dusk is something to enjoy. Though there is no flower garden I have a good many Italian pots with leafy plants, fuchsias, begonias, tuberoses, geraniums, etc. By the time they are all watered and shifted into the sun or out of the wind, forth and back, I feel that it may be as well that I have no digging garden! A little herb garden, which is too shaded to flourish as it should, does well enough to keep us supplied with chives, parsley, taragon and mint. I prefer to think that in ceasing to kick against pricks I have come to a contented enjoyment of my planting.

Those Unsightly Shrubs

Sarah R. Childs

NEARLY everyone in this area has pruning problems except the people who live in new ranch houses, and theirs are yet to come.

Our plantings, here, are mostly well established and many of the individual shrubs have lost any semblance of fulfilling their original function in the landscape. They have become leggy, top heavy, intergrown with others and are a liability rather than an asset.

The reason for this is that they weren't pruned properly when they were small and that it takes drastic action and courage to tackle them when they do get out of hand.

Pruning seems to be considered an occult science by a great many people, but there are some basic rules of thumb that anyone can follow.

The *reason* for pruning is to keep the shrub in an attractive shape and to produce as many blossoms as possible.

The *time* for pruning — a most important factor — is right after the shrub has bloomed. This is an easy rule to remember — but there is one exception. Shrubs that bloom *after* July should be pruned in late winter or early spring. The reason for this is that the flower buds form on new wood — so the late bloomers should be pruned to make them throw as much new wood as possible.

Always make cuts immediately above a side branch or bud. This will avoid a lot of ugly stubs which will decay and harbor disease and insects.

Use a tree wound paint on any cuts that are more than an inch in diameter.

Old neglected shrubs are the hardest to cope with — or, at least, the most discouraging. These same rules apply, but you just have to be much more drastic and put in a lot more work.

First — Remove all dead wood.

Second — Remove one third of the old wood at the ground, choosing the oldest and the most unsightly canes.

Third — Remove weak shoots and thin the twiggy areas.

Fourth — Pull all the debris away, stand back and view it with a critical eye.

This rejuvenating process is going to take three years, so don't be either too discouraged or too drastic.

By now, you can at least see what you have. You may, and probably will, still have an awkward looking shrub. If so, cut a little more but *not* to the ground level. Instead, cut a few branches to the first or second side shoot and the leggy shoots or twiggy tops to a side bud. Later on in the season you can pinch some of the tips — especially in the case of viburnums, cotoneasters, Japanese barberry and snowberry.

If, the next year, you find that you have overpruned and, as a result, stimulated the growth of too many new shoots from the crown, cut some of these off leaving only a few of the sturdiest canes to take the place of the old ones you removed the year before.

Broad-leaved evergreens are a more difficult problem because they will not grow new branches as deciduous shrubs will. It is best to avoid pruning these if possible.

Pinching the new growth on yews and other fine-needled evergreens will make them bushier and can be done throughout the season. Occasionally it is necessary to cut some of the branches back about eight to ten inches to stimulate new growth, usually in the center.

Never prune yews or hedges so that they are broader at the top than at the bottom. This results in all the lower growth dying from lack of sun. The top may look lovely but the rest of the bush will be unsightly.

I can tell others what to do, but, often, when I prune my own shrubs, I find that each one is an exception to all these rules. It is only my conviction that it is necessary that makes me persevere.

However when I am completely defeated by a bush, I have another solution. I cut it to the ground, paint the stump with tree poison, and, if the resultant gap is not an improvement — which it often is — I go to the nearest nursery for a replacement.

We cherish our old shrubs, maybe because they've always been there or "why not use what we have?" But sometimes it's a question of just how desirable "what we have" is. The newer shrubs usually have been developed to have a more attractive habit of growth, blossoms which are not only more numerous, but of more attractive shades, and a greater disease resistance.

However — these new bushes will need a yearly pruning too — so your pruning problems will still be with you but in a more manageable form.

Daffodils

Gertrude B. McCarthy

DAFFODILS have inspired poets from Shakespeare to Wordsworth to Amy Lowell. Indeed, is there any more delightful and heart-warming sight than daffodils in the early spring when most other plants are still dormant? Their bloom is not only conclusive proof that the long winter is past, but they also have the attractive quality of being very easy to grow. Any location in full sun or in shade is suitable as long as *some* sun reaches it.

Daffodils are equally lovely naturalized in drifts at the edge of a meadow or a woodland, or planted in clumps beside a natural pool, in front of a gray stone wall, among broad-leaved evergreens, or on a steep bank where it may be difficult to grow grass. They can also be planted in pockets in the rock-garden, using small bulbs such as grape hyacinths, scillas, and fritillarias to accent them.

When the daffodils have finished blooming, their blossoms must be cut off and their foliage left to die down. This presents no problem in a meadow or woodland, but it does produce definite mowing difficulties on a lawn. In flower borders it is possible to grow the daffodils a little way back in the bed and so have room to plant some annuals or geraniums in front of them to hide the dying foliage.

In this climate the bulbs should be planted no later than September. August is a good time for separating and transplanting. It is wise to mark clumps that need transplanting before the foliage disappears.

Bone meal is essential to the growth of daffodils, one application before blooming, a second in mid-summer and a third in the autumn is recommended. If possible keep well watered until the foliage has turned yellow.

What is the difference between a daffodil and a narcissus? Parkinson says, "Many idle and ignorant gardeners . . . doe call some of the Daffodils, Narcissus, when, as all that know any Latine, know that Narcissus is the Latine name and Daffodill the English of one and the same thing." This seems clear enough; however, there are many classifications of Narcissus (Daffodils), with a great number of varieties in each class. Catalogues from Max Schling or Scheepers of New York, De Jager of South Hamilton, Mass., White Flower Farm, Litchfield, Conn., or George Park Seed Co., Greenwood, South Carolina, show very good pictures and give descriptions to help you choose the varieties you want for a succession of bloom.

In the general order of blooming the yellow, white and bi-color trumpets come first, then yellow and bi-color Incomparabiles, Barrii in yellow and white, and Leedsii which are all pure white, triandus hybrids, cyclamineus hybrids, jonquilla hybrids, poeta and double daffodils in white and yellow.

Excellent varieties for this area in their order of blooming are: Music Hall, King Alfred, Mrs. Backhouse, Texas, Beersheba, Mt. Hood, Semper Avante, Thalia, and Cheerfulness.

Bibliography:

WISTER, Gertrude S., *The Hardy Garden Bulbs*, E. P. Dutton & Co., Inc., 1964.

•

Growing Roses North of the Merrimack

E. Raymond Childs
Dover, N. H.

CYNTHIA Westcott very tersely states, as the title to one of her splendid books, "Anyone Can Grow Roses." I would add, for the benefit of those who have never grown roses in New England, a few subtitles, e.g., "They do not grow themselves," or "If you will follow a Few Simple Rules," or "If You Love Roses." Those of us who have grown roses north of the Merrimack River know only too well that there are many discouraging hours and many disappointments during the twelve perplexing and unpredictable months that comprise the northern New England year. But the rewards are so great and the personal satisfaction is so complete when we look on our garden of lush, healthy rose bushes with their colorful and beautiful blossoms, that we easily forget the anxious hours and decide that growing roses really is fun and well worth the extra effort.

For the embryonic rosarian I strongly recommend a humble beginning with six to twelve bushes as a test run, a test of your patience and interest and a test of the suitability of your property for a rose garden. Of paramount importance for the best growing conditions are plenty of sunshine (at least eight hours) and good rich soil with adequate drainage. Roses abhor wet feet in summer and ice in winter. The addition of well rotted manure, quantities of bone meal, and compost to the garden soil are desirable. The rose bed(s) should be prepared at least two or three weeks before planting.

In buying rose bushes it is important to select good sturdy stock from a reliable nursery, where they will have spent about two years growing under climatic conditions as similar to ours as possible. I have found that the nurseries in New England, New York and Pennsylvania best fill this bill. The 'bargain bushes' from Texas just do not do well in New England. An especially hardy strain for winter survival comes from the Brownell's in Little Compton, R. I., and are known as sub-zero roses, but there are many of the regular patented hybrid teas, floribunda, and climbers which come through our winters nicely. Some that I have had in New Hampshire for more than ten years are New Dawn (cl.), Blaze (cl.), Climbing Summer Snow (cl.), Frau Karl Druschki (h.t.), Rubaiyat (h.t.), Peace (h.t.), Garnet (flori.), Fashion (flori.), Spartan (flori. 8 years). However, it is not always safe to assume that a rose from one garden will do as well in another. Conditions for growing are never exactly the same in one garden as in another garden, and one has to resort to the trial and error method over the years. Complete planting instructions are furnished with the bushes from the nurseries and should be followed carefully. Advocates of spring planting or fall planting are about equally divided, but I prefer spring planting in this climate. In the spring we can assess the amount of winter damage and do our replacing as well as new planting at the same time.

Planting will have been completed by the end of April. New growth starts early in May, and the first blooming comes toward the end of June, usually reaching its height during the first two weeks of July. From then on until a hard freeze we get intermittent bloom from the hybrid teas and more or less constant blooming from the floribunda. Feeding is recommended about June first and again about July fifteenth, never later for this climate as we do not want too much new growth going into the fall. There are many good commercial fertilizers available. Scratch them into the surface of the soil, not too deeply, as roses have shallow roots and do not like to be disturbed. Plenty of water is necessary during the summer, but water deeply each time (about once a week). Regular spraying and/or dusting is necessary to keep insects, mites and disease under control, but a strong word of caution about the use of these materials. Most of them are very dangerous to man as well as to insects and disease, and directions on the packages must be followed explicitly. Also keep the materials in the original containers, so that the directions may be checked each time they are used. It can be extremely hazardous to trust a faulty memory on this score. To mulch or not to mulch is a matter of personal preference. The main advantage of a mulch is a neater looking bed, partial discouragement of weeds, and longer maintenance of moisture in the soil. No major pruning is usually necessary during the summer. That is done mostly in spring, and the use of good sharp instruments is recommended. Many excellent books are available on the subject of rose culture, and at least one or two should be in every gardener's library.

Winter care for roses in this climate is of tremendous importance. After several severe frosts and before the ground is hard frozen some time in November, it is necessary to mound up dirt around each bush to ten or twelve inches. This dirt may have to be brought in for the purpose. It is also well to strip off all the leaves from the bushes before the 'hilling' is done. Extra long canes should be shortened to prevent their whipping about in the winter winds, and a cover of pine boughs placed over the entire bed *after* the ground is *frozen* hard. This winter protection should not be disturbed until spring when new growth has started and the new shoots are approximately one inch long.

Now you have gone through a growing season and if you breathe a sigh of relief you might just as well stop there. Chances are, however, that you will spend many happy winter hours poring over the colorful rose catalogs and planning the expansion of the original 'test' bed. I have never yet had enough room for all the plants I wanted. There is a lure about the new roses that is hard to resist, and every garden should have a few of the old roses, moss, shrub, etc. I have had a York and Lancaster for fifteen years and it always provokes conversation during its heavy blooming in late June. Membership in the New England Rose Society, the American Rose Society and the Maine Rose Society in Portland will bring an added enjoyment to the growing of roses, and before long you are a real rosarian with real pride and satisfaction in your garden. From here the steps to a rewarding collection of show ribbons is a natural and an easy one.

Shrub Roses

Cynthia Westcott,
Croton-on-Hudson, New York

ALL roses are shrubs, defined by Webster as low, usually several stemmed woody plants. Most rosarians, however, think of shrub roses as being larger and having a different habit from hybrid teas and floribundas that are ordinarily planted in beds. To me, shrub roses are those that can be used as accent or background in the same way that we plant forsythia or lilacs. Some shrub roses, like lilacs, have only one period of bloom; others repeat at intervals during the summer; and a few have fairly continuous bloom.

I don't know which shrub roses are best adapted to the varying climates of Maine. All I can do is to tell you of a few that I grow and love (and that have survived very severe winters in the suburban New York areas) hoping that most of them will also thrive somewhere "from the Merrimack to the Kennebec."

Species roses are indisputably shrubs and the one that blooms earliest for me is *Rosa hugonis*, the lovely yellow single known as Father Hugo's rose. The trick in growing this is to withhold the usual amenities associated with rose culture. Put it in poor soil and do not fertilize. I twice lost *R. hugonis* in my New Jersey garden because the plants were too close to other rose bushes being regularly fed. Here at Springvale it blooms in barren soil near a rock ledge.

The next rose to bloom in my garden is FRÜHLINGSMORGEN, a large, graceful shrub with most attractive blue-green foliage. The blooms, formed all along the canes, are single with soft cherry pink petals, yellow at the center, and maroon stamens. Frühlingsmorgen in full flower is utter delight. My bush does not repeat but, because of the fine foliage, looks well in summer and, towards autumn, has stunning red hips, crab-apple size and shape.

Next comes AGNES, a tall hybrid rugosa. The yellow buds, on short stems along stiff, prickly canes, open to very double, large, creamy yellow flowers that are extremely fragrant, also long-lasting if cut for the house. Agnes stays in bloom for nearly a month and about midway is joined by VANGUARD, another hybrid rugosa. Both roses have rugose (wrinkled) foliage but that of Agnes is dull while that of Vanguard is very glossy. Vanguard's flowers are large, double, salmon-pink, very fragrant. There is no repeat bloom but the display lasts nearly four weeks and after that the handsome foliage makes this a good background shrub. Allow plenty of room — Vanguard may grow as tall and as wide as a climber — but don't bother with spraying.

FRAU DAGMAR HARTOPP is a low rugosa that does repeat its satiny pink, five-petaled flowers all season. PINK GROOTENDORST is taller, has clusters of small, double, rosy pink flowers with fringed petals. They look exactly like tiny carnations. There is profuse bloom in June, some the following months.

There are two hybrid musk roses that are very similar, having small flowers in great trusses, willowy arching canes, and shiny foliage with seven leaflets. Soft pink BELINDA is sold as a shrub. Dark pink to cherry red ROBIN HOOD is sold as a hedge rose, on its own roots, but it could also be used as a specimen shrub. Both bloom repeatedly through the season. OTTO LINNE is a cross between Robin Hood and a polyantha. It is a bush of medium height with hybrid musk foliage and small, dark pink flowers in large polyantha clusters.

THE FAIRY is our best-known example of a shrub polyantha and this is the rose I recommend to all beginning gardeners. It is not fussy about soil, almost never requires spraying, and can be used as a specimen shrub, in a hedge, flanking entrances, or on banks, provided you allow it enough room. The Fairy first spreads horizontally to five or six feet, then fills in the center three or four feet high. It starts blooming rather late but then continues its clusters of charming small pink flowers (much like a miniature Dorothy Perkins) unceasingly until long after first frost. The small, shiny, dark green leaves are most attractive and almost never succumb to mildew. In midsummer heat the pink flowers fade almost to white but in cool Maine there should be less loss of color. The Fairy is excellent for arrangements.

And now The Fairy has a rival, hybrid polyantha SEA FOAM, introduced in the fall of 1964 by the Conard-Pyle Company (West Grove, Pennsylvania). It, too, is a carefree shrub, spreading six to eight feet as a specimen bush, covered with foamy white clusters of medium-sized flowers. Its willowy canes may be tied up to make a climber along a fence or can weep down over a bank, with dark green, lustrous foliage and continuing bloom.

Almost all hybrid perpetual roses can be used as hardy specimen shrubs or as background bushes. My favorite is HENRY NEVARD with its huge, dark red, very double, very fragrant flowers and pleasing dark green foliage. After a magnificent June display there is intermittent bloom until frost. BARONESS ROTHSCHILD is a soft rosy pink hybrid perpetual that repeats some for me but not as reliably as Henry Nevard.

Long classed as a hybrid perpetual, now unfortunately listed as a hybrid tea, FRAU KARL DRUSCHKI becomes a huge shrub, six to eight feet high and wide, with hundreds of blooms in June, a fair number recurrently summer and fall. The large, double, pure white flower is so pure in form it often wins Queen of Show. Henry Nevard, Frau Karl Druschki and similar roses need moderate pruning in spring and some cutting back during the summer to keep them producing.

Also listed as a hybrid tea but very definitely a shrub requiring lots of room is lovely GOLDEN WINGS, covered with large, single, pale yellow flowers, opening from pointed golden buds. This bush is reliably hardy for me and I let it grow without much pruning back.

Where climate allows high pruning other, more conventional hybrid teas may also be grown separately as shrubs. PEACE, planted by itself and only moderately pruned, becomes a big bush. Pink and gold CHICAGO PEACE is even more gorgeous than its parent and LUCKY PIECE is almost as good. Bright rose PINK PEACE does not resemble PEACE in form of flower or glossy foliage but it makes a fine large bush with continual production of very fragrant flowers. CANDY STRIPE is a charming striped variation of Pink Peace, with slightly more restrained growth.

Pink grandiflora QUEEN ELIZABETH makes an excellent shrub rose, growing four or five feet wide, six feet tall if allowed sufficient space. Not so tall but very hardy, vigorous and everblooming is grandiflora JOHN S. ARMSTRONG with its very dark red velvety flowers of camellia form. The buds are so black visitors often ask if they have been hit by frost, but it is their natural color.

Most floribunda roses are preferred in beds, or in groups in perennial borders, or as hedges, or outlining hybrid tea beds. BETTY PRIOR, however, is large enough to stand alone and makes a fine specimen shrub, pruned only enough to remove winter injury. I had a bush in my New Jersey garden large enough for a cardinal to nest in unafraid, even though it was right beside a path in continuous use. Betty Prior is another rose you can plant and forget. I never spray mine.

Not exactly a shrub but a rose I hope you will try in Maine is climber CITY OF YORK. It is a once bloomer and for this reason the introducers (Conard-Pyle Company) dropped the rose from their list because of too few sales. I have, however, persuaded them to bud it again for 1965. Pale yellow buds open to semi-double, white, intensely fragrant flowers with lovely yellow stamens. There are a few flowers the first year and thousands succeeding years, the display lasting nearly a month. After that, the glossy green foliage makes a most attractive background. City of York can cover a fence or a bank. Here at Springvale my bush does both. Set in a shelf cut into the bank, half of the climber is trained up over an iron railing, the other half makes a ground cover extending about fifteen feet over the slope. I have never sprayed City of York nor have I had to prune it much after severe winters.

There are, of course, many shrub roses to try in Maine, including the native species, such as *Rosa blanda, R. carolina, R. palustris* and *R. virginiana*, that flourish from Canada southwards. Sources of old shrub and species roses include Will Tillotson's Roses, Watsonville, California, and Joseph J. Kern Nursery, Mentor, Ohio.

Why Not Grow Roses as Annuals?

Sarah R. Childs

ROSES can be hardy, with proper winter care, in much of the area between the Merrimack and the Kennebec. However, there are some locations where the temperature goes too low or the frost too deep, so that it is either impossible, or very uncertain, that roses will survive the winter or, what is often more fatal, the spring.

Another hazard is that faced by summer residents, who are not here to mound the bushes up after the ground is frozen in the fall, or to uncover them at the right time in the spring.

For rose lovers faced with these problems, growing roses as annuals is a solution. If the bushes *should* survive an especially propitious winter, that is just so much to the good.

Whenever I have suggested using roses as annuals, the answer has always been "But they are too expensive!"

I don't think that they need to be. Dormant roses from the chain stores can be bought very cheaply. Roses from Texas and bargain assortments are not expensive. These might often be a poor investment for a permanent rose garden. They usually have no guarantee, are grown under different weather conditions from ours in Northern New England, and may not have been kept properly moist. However, if, when purchased, they show signs of life, they will survive for, at least, one season.

These can be bought for under a dollar apiece. A flat of annuals costs around seventy-five cents. Six rose bushes, with their beauty and distinction, will cover, more effectively, the same area that six or more flats of pansies, petunias, zinnias, etc., will.

Cutting off the dead-heads of annuals is a practically endless chore. A few roses can be made into a lovely flower arrangement, usually with far more distinction than one made with a mass of conventional annuals.

I would rather have the roses!

Irrigation of Roses

Josephine Johaneson

SUMMER has come to Maine.

Gone are those unpredictable spring days when winter dies hard, waking in the morning to frost on the lawn, fearful of damage to tender buds— prayerful that all has not been uncovered too early.

Gone are those hours of exacting, back-breaking "MUSTS" against time and weather — spraying and more spraying — pruning and evaluating winter damage — replacements of old favorites and the exciting addition of new roses.

Summer is here and you look forward to a harvest of beauty in your rose garden.

Already the established roses are blooming, the newly planted replacements have sent up strong canes, and the first buds are beginning to form.

Only two problems now confront you — spraying and watering.

Spraying is a question of conditions and experience. Watering is even as important to the health of your roses.

With the following simple system of irrigation this can be cut down to a minimum of labor, and at the same time produce a maximum of water required to keep the soil cool and damp, irrespective of summer conditions.

An investment in enough green ribbon hoses to water your entire rose bed adequately is an investment well worth while. The hoses can be used season after season if taken up in the fall, and cared for. Ribbon hose comes in several lengths — use more of the shorter lengths if it suits your garden better. Lay this hose watering side down between each row of rose bushes — you can even bend it around a bush or corner. However, the fewer bends in your hose the more effective the flow of water. Be sure the nozzles of these hoses are placed nearest your water supply.

Before continuing with the next step it is well to test your irrigation system by attaching your garden hose to two of the ribbon hoses by using a V shaped attachment that can be bought at any hardware store. Turn the faucet so the water runs gently through the entire length of the ribbon hose. Too much force will cause erosion around the rose roots, whereas a gentle seepage will penetrate to the depth desired. To keep the hoses in place strong wire can be cut in the shape of small wickets to loop over the hose and pin it to the ground, thus it becomes a permanent system throughout the summer months.

The last step is to spread at least two inches of mulch over the entire garden — the mulch used is a matter of choice. Not only will the mulch keep the soil cool and moist, it will prevent weeds and fallen rose leaves from contaminating the soil should black spots appear.

A good watering once a week is all that is required. A gentle seepage of eight hours or so should penetrate to the depth of one foot. If your rose bed enjoys good drainage a little over watering once a week is better than casual watering when the busy gardener can get around to it. To test the gage of watering, take a stake such as is used to tie up delphinium, push this into the ground and you can tell by the feel how deep the moisture has penetrated.

Like all experiences pertaining to gardening, one learns most by trial and error, what works in one case may not work in another, conditions varying as they do.

I first saw a system of irrigation used in an extensive rose garden belonging to a friend who was an experienced and fine rosarian. It was a far more elaborate layout of piping and centrally controlled valves than I needed for my modest rose garden. I eliminated the piping and valves by using my garden hoses from several nearby faucets.

After three years of simple experimenting in irrigation I still find there is much to learn. Last summer it was gratifying that Black Spot was almost nonexistent in spite of unusually foggy days and damp nights.

Water is only one of the problems of producing fine specimens, but it is nice to go to bed at night, knowing your roses are being irrigated, while you sleep.

Potted Roses

WHEN you arrive in June at your summer home and find your rose bed looking rather scrawny with gaps here and there, and it is too late to order dormant bushes, do not despair! Potted Roses will come to your aid.

These helpful answers to a gardener's prayer are readily available from nearly any nursery or greenhouse and come in all stages of growth, from plants with the leaf buds just breaking to those in full bloom. They are in excellent old stand-by varieties with a good choice of colors.

Be sure to choose plants with a few strong canes, and ones that are budded low. That is, with the knob that indicates the union between graft and understock as near the top of the pot as possible. This means that you won't have to dig as deep a hole — in rocky soil this is important.

Do not plant pot and all unless it is "Fertile Potted," in which case it all goes in. Dig a good large hole that will allow the graft to be an inch underground, set the plant in the hole, tear away the paper pot, fill with rich soil well firmed and watered in and there you are, with a rose bed in full bloom and no setback. In fact, in this area with its short growing season it seems sensible to make much more use of potted roses and have many weeks of bloom.

Bushes grown in this way can also be transferred to ornamental pots and placed wherever they are most effective. M. P. H.

A Terrace Garden

Alice H. Rollins

THERE is a limited amount of land connected with my house, and none of it is quite suitable for a garden. This is probably fortunate because my thumb is not a green one, but I enjoy flowers and plants.

A small flagstone terrace which opens off the living room offered possibilities. Here there is ledge upon which the house is situated. After two futile efforts, at which times putting in annuals was a failure, I decided my garden would have to be potted material. This proved to be the answer, and a most satisfactory one.

Each year I try different plants. Geraniums are my favorite (Enchantress is a good pink variety), but fuchsia and various types of begonias and roses are equally enchanting. Last summer, an experimental garnet rose bush in a pot did very well, blooming throughout most of the season.

Browallia, strawberry plants, pansies and chrysanthemums can add beauty to a terrace. Five or seven petunias in tubs can give a gay spot of color to enhance the effect of a garden without a garden. Many kinds of ivy can be used, which make a pleasing background and can also be planted in hanging pots or baskets. The chances are if you get an outdoor ivy it will do well, as mine has, and stay green all summer. Then it can be brought into the house for winter decoration.

Some of the plants can be removed from the terrace when they cease to be attractive. They can be cut back, put out of sight and brought out again when they start to bud. The local greenhouses have proved very useful in suggesting appropriate material. They will have ideas for plants that do well in shady spots, or in sunny places. They can tell you when and how long they will bloom.

A shell-shaped bird bath, resting on stones surrounded by a lush growth of periwinkle, gives a cool looking and pleasing point of interest.

My terrace is gay and it is always a challenge to discover different plants and try out new ideas. All in all this is a most rewarding solution for my need to have color and plants outside the house. The pots can be as delightful as the flowers in them if one chooses to stray away from the ordinary variety. There are many attractive containers that can be bought and used to advantage.

This type of gardening, if it can be called such, is not for those who love to dig in the soil. As we grow older, maybe digging, weeding and planting does not have the appeal it once had. From necessity, the desire for a garden and not having a proper place for one, was met. Gardening without a garden can be fun. It's easy and restful to one's aching back and I recommend it to all who have the same problems I did.

Amaryllis from Andirons

Eleanor Johnston

YEARS ago, long before we acquired our home in York, the house next door burned down. It must have been a proper fire for nothing was left and the site became a hayfield so overgrown with weeds and pea vine that not even a depression was evident. Imagine our surprise when the hay was cut and there emerged the stone foundation and cellar hole of the erstwhile house. Our initial reaction was shock for the hole was some 30 by 40 feet in area and a good 9 feet deep. The floor was littered with rusty bed springs, stoves in variety, andirons in quantity, in short, all the unburnables that had fallen from above at the time of the fire. The shock turned to pleased surprise when we discovered that the foundation walls were of nice granite blocks of random shapes and sizes. Obviously here was a ready made spot for a sunken garden.

The hole was filled to within 18 inches of the top, the center seeded and plants set out in 3-foot borders next the wall. For some years everything throve. The delphiniums, phlox, lilies and chrysanthemums were spectacular. But, alas, there was no shelter to protect them from the west winds blowing unhindered across the adjacent golf links. Eventually all the tall things were abandoned in favor of low-growing alpine and rock garden types of plants which show off to good advantage the gray stone walls behind them. Veronicas, astilbes, artemesias, achilleas, candytuft, etc. provide variety in form and color of foliage. They are not blown about and they do not seem to mind the York winters. On top of the wall, so that they drip over in spots, the alpine *Arenaria laricifolia* and various kinds of thymes break the severity of the top course of the wall.

Another thirty years have passed and the only flower left from the original garden is an *Amaryllis Halli*, the bulb bought at a five and ten! Every spring the strap-like leaves come up in increasing numbers, die down in June and disappear. Then with a regularity as reliable as the swallows of Capistrano, on August 5th the buds break ground, and by the 15th the " naked ladies " are in full bloom. A late spring or early, a hot summer or a cold one, nothing seems to affect their passion for promptness. We think they must be nourished by the bedsprings, stoves and andirons still rusting in the cellar hole beneath them.

A Meadow Garden

Penelope W. Hyde,
Bedford, N. Y.

WHEN my husband and I inherited our house in Kittery ten years ago, it had not been lived in for three seasons, and before that only during the summers. The true gardener of the house had died eight years earlier. Nothing had since been done in the garden, except cutting the grass path that surrounded a meadow, and a patch of lawn that faced Old Ferry Lane.

It was early June when we first confronted the house, dusty and damp after so many years of neglect. Soap and water and fresh paint could work wonders with it. But what about the garden — how could we put that into any sort of order? And then how could we keep it in shape? Each year we would be in Kittery only a short summer, and living at a considerable distance the other ten months. As we pushed open the door on the water side of the house, we were full of memories of the old garden, and fearful to look at what was left of it.

Instead of a pathetic tangle, imagine our surprise to find a field full of flowers reaching to the water's edge! Wildflowers of the Maine roadside were mingling with flowers that had escaped the old garden's bounds of cultivation. Not in ten years of good gardening could we have created such a *millefleurs* of tapestry as we saw running out to the sea that stretched blue and beautiful to the Isles of Shoals and beyond!

Shrubs and plants that demanded attention had long since disappeared — all except the hardy ones with a strong desire to live and propagate. But what a field day they had had! The Russell lupines, pink, blue and white, had spread from the now vanished garden into the meadow facing the sea. The tall blue-and-white veronica had done likewise. Lemon day lilies were everywhere. The air was fragrant with the scent of lilacs, now nearly twenty feet high and giving the old house privacy from the neighbors. Apple trees beside the water were coming into bloom. A wistaria tree, twisted by the winter winds into a Japanese bonsai shape, was covered with pendulous bunches of fragrant white blossoms. On the edge of the meadow near the house, flowering almonds were in bloom. A viburnum Carlesii was full and sweet despite one of Maine's coldest winters. The tenacity of the roses surprised us most. Harrisons, Madame Plantiers and Madame Hardys were covered with buds, although without benefit of pruning, and the sweetbriars and rugosas had multiplied as if they were native to the State of Maine.

A meadow of flowers needing no cultivation whatever! Here was the key to the perfect garden for us, who tended during most of the growing year, our cultivated beds on a farm in Westchester County, New York. From that moment we knew we had found the answer for our summer garden.

Each year has added to our knowledge and delight. Our expeditions upcountry or by sea yield plants we have dug up, or sometimes honestly bought from a nursery, to grace the home meadow. Our good compost heaps are enjoyed equally by the flowers of the field and of the garden. Our weeding is minimum because the whole meadow is a living ground-cover. Where we need mulch around the roses or a newly planted tree or shrub, we use unfinished compost. Every fall we cut down the meadow flowers and the grass, to protect against fire, to keep the chokecherries and other saplings in bounds, to produce healthy growth, and to start new compost.

Pruning and mowing are placed firmly in the hands of a professional gardener. Although children and guests may be willing to cut the grass, the paths grow not straight but narrow under their administration. We like our paths wide enough for two people to walk abreast, with room enough for a grandchild or a dog besides.

Other people's gardens, nurseries, and the University of New Hampshire's experiment station are sources of interest and knowledge. From our farm we bring potted plants, potted trees and hanging baskets to brighten the Kittery porch and terrace. When planting, we concentrate on trees and shrubs that will be in bloom when we are in residence. And we study nature, to see how she combines her flowers — and find her taste impeccable. What is lovelier in August than orange day lilies and deep blue monkshood that we found side by side in our own meadow!

Among my own greatest joys from this garden are bouquets brought into the house. For these I use flowers from the meadow combined with vines, berries and leaves.

So our stay in Maine is never troubled with gardening problems. Our meadow is always an area of delight for us. And it answers the question how to have a summer garden without really gardening.

Here is a partial list of trees, shrubs and plants grown successfully in the Kittery garden:

TREES

Fruit trees — Apple and Pear	Copper Beech (This is quite inappropriate
Arborvitae	but we cannot resist its charm.)
Yew	

SHRUBS

Flowering Almond	Smoke Bush
Spiraea	Juniper (We like the wild ones)
Viburnum	Bayberries
Philadelphus	Roses, climbing, old-fashioned Sweetbriars, Rugosas
Weigela, Bristol Ruby	and the Brownell collection.

VINES

Roses, New Dawn, Crimson Rambler
Honeysuckle
Clematis Jackmanii

Grapes, Concord
Matrimony Vine
Wistaria (in form of tree)

PLANTS

Asters, all we can find and buy
Astilbe
Monkshood (escape from old garden)
Day lilies, all Rondi
Turk's Cap lilies and Canadense
Veronica (escape from old garden)
Funkia, hosta, both blue and white
Yarrow, both wild and cultivated varieties
Cranes Bills
Chickory
Iris (Blue Flags)
Lupines (Russell escapes from old garden)

Golden Rod (all kinds)
Paeonia (gone wild)
Poke
Climbing false buckwheat
Bladder Campion
Rock Cress
Black Snake Weed
Cinquefoil
Pasture Rose
Black Cherry, choke
Buckwheat (family — all varieties)

Humor in Humus

Harriet Robeson

THE allure of alliteration is manifest in this title. It came out of the blue and has me nailed to the mast because humus is my problem. It is one of the most ill-defined words in gardening lexicon — its variations have a colossal range, each one with something added to or eliminated from.

The title of this soliloquy begins happily for "Humor" is a happy word. One immediately anticipates a delightful experience; a mood that is relaxing, mellow, and for the most part kindly; it evokes a smile. Not like wit which is generally meant to be trenchant, laugh-provoking and often may wound.

However, "Humus" is another story — "produced by the decomposition of vegetable or animal matter." I suppose a real "dirt gardener" can wax ecstatic over decayed matter. Of course if I could prove my prize lily is due to its sitting in some rotted leaf mold I might too become elated. But here is an illustration of my perpetual quandary. You don't use decayed matter for lilies. One authority says to plant the bulbs on sand and the next authority says, "never — no sand." So there you are! Confusion!

My friends never mention anything pertaining to their gardens but humus is the common denominator. So feeling depressingly ignorant and far from able to discuss gardening in any phase, I purchase a 744 page book on gardening.

36

I turn at once to humus. After careful perusal of three long involved paragraphs I come to understand that humus is a necessary component of good soil. It provides water-holding capacity, stimulates plant growth, and adds mineral nutrients, etc., etc. If it's sandy soil it needs humus. If it's clayey soil it needs humus. Humus there must be! Well, I have that settled!

Next, where do I get humus? It being decomposed matter it seems as if a manure pile would be a likely source. Do you know in my new garden book there are twelve kinds of manure? In my childhood manure meant the droppings of our one horse, carefully garnered and rotted by our one man. How do I know which of the twelve manures is best for my garden? — if I can get it — and which flower needs more-or-less of nitrogen, phosphorus or potassium of which each of the twelve manures has a different percentage — manure is too complicated for me.

Undaunted I search further to find peat (God bless it) is a source of humus — all its rotting done and dried! I strongly suspect peat will provide my future humus since leaf mold and compost piles seem far afield. Then the acid content of soil may prove to be a problem. How do I know if my soil is under acid or over acid or which plant hungers for acid? And when do I mulch or not mulch and which of the many do I mulch with?

I don't remember all this falderal as a child. Flowers just grew. I never was very enthusiastic about them because I had a daily stint. One day two long rows of sweet peas had to be picked, and the next a quarter mile of nasturtiums along a wall. Passersby admired them, but not I! No beach with my brothers, no sail, no catching of fiddler crabs for fishing, no swim until those pesky flowers were plucked. My brothers got paid for digging clams and for the fish they caught — if cleaned — but I never got a nickel for the thousands upon thousands of flowers I picked through the years. Justice??? My tepid enthusiasm for gardens died!

Not until fifty years later when I become a Piscataqua Garden Club member do I ponder a garden of my own. After fifteen years of struggle, however, I admit defeat. Now the mind is slowing, the knees are buckling and my associates are so learned in techniques and so superb in results that I can only stand and gape. I don't like to stand and gape!

If I hadn't marked up my expensive garden book I would return it. I've made a decision. In future I intend to plant my garden in petunias which like Topsy just grow.

Humor in Humus? I can't find it!

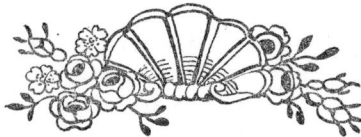

Rock Gardens in Maine

Betty Jane Hayward,
Scarborough, Maine

THE group of plants familiarly called Rock Plants should correctly be known as Alpine Plants. Mountains are the native habitat of even the common and well-known sorts.

Geographically and Geologically, Maine is particularly adapted to growing these species successfully, They originate in cool and rocky areas. Our cool Summer temperature, the emergence of rock everywhere, moisture from the Sea and Mountains, plus the consistent snowcover in Winter provide the desirable conditions.

Accommodating mountain plants to sea-level conditions had its origin in Europe little more than one hundred years ago. Fifty years would perhaps cover the period since rock-gardening became popular in the United States. As with other novel introductions it became a craze; the result was some poor examples in dooryards, rock standing on end, little thought to the requirements and habits of the plants themselves. Fortunately, serious gardeners soon grouped together and formed The American Rock Garden Society in 1934. Today, there are many attractive gardens in evidence, the poor ones have all disappeared.

During the last decade these dwarf plants have come into wide usefulness, particularly the spreading and more easily grown types, while specialists derive pleasure and profit in growing the rare kinds from the world's mountains. Today's trend to suburban living, and the building of homes in wooded and sometimes rocky situations make it necessary to bring all areas into the general landscaping plan.

Rock-walls are often the answer to leveling the grounds around a property. Patios have replaced porches everywhere. Out-cropping ledges, skillfully exposed and planted, become a natural and attractive feature in the picture. The sloping bank is the ideal spot for a rock garden. In all these places rock-plants and low shrubs are the appropriate material for planting.

The success of any planting is dependent on care in preparation, drainage, soil depth and fertility. Ledges to be planted must be cleaned of old soil to rock surface and filled with fresh supply, firmly pressed in. Rock-walls can be planned with pockets filled with soil in the process of building, and plants introduced at once.

Rock gardens look more natural if large stones can be used in construction to simulate a ledge effect. Crevices between make ideal locations for planting. The rock garden proper with its hill, dale and plateau supplies every desirable aspect for Alpines, of all sorts.

The patio accommodates the various low and spreading kinds that can be trod upon, small bits planted between the flag-stones or slate will in a short time spread out to fill the spaces. In preparing, it is advised to use good soil, enriched and rather firm. Gravel or sand washes up onto the stone, it supplies little for the plants to grow on, and is untidy after rain. All the varieties of *Thymus serpyllum* are desirable. *Arenaria verna*, and *A. verna aurea*, very low and grasslike, spangled with tiny, white flowers. Other low types are suitable. Occasionally, at one side, away from traffic a plant of dwarf Dianthus looks well.

Rock-walls afford opportunity for much attractive and permanent planting, the perfect drainage and cool rootrun among the stones, assure long life to plants that frequently die elsewhere. Examples are *Alyssum saxatile* and its variety *A. saxatile citrinum*, *Aubrieta*, *Arabis* and the so-called Creeping Phlox, *P. subulata*. Masses of Sempervivum fit naturally between the stones, and the flat growing *Cotoneaster addpressa* will cover a large area eventually, creeping in and out, clinging closely as it goes.

Rock gardens, whether natural or constructed, provide homes for a vast number of beautiful and interesting plants. Here the gardener can give vent to his enthusiasm and talent. Lovely effects in color harmony and mass planting are possible. Drifts of yellow, blue and soft pink and lavender in all the chosen rock plants are a joy. Select specimens of the rarer kinds go into specially reserved places. Perhaps these two aspects possible in rock gardening are contributing factors in its popularity, a garden of lovely color, pleasing in itself, and the opportunity to please oneself in attempting to grow some of the world's rare plants from faraway places.

Shade is a necessary consideration for many of the desirable plants we all wish to grow successfully. Primulas as a group require some shadow for a part of the day, Gentians appreciate coolness, as do many other mountain natives. Continual sunshine at sea level is quite different from conditions in the heights. A shaded path among trees is ideal for these favored plants. Here too, the choice native wildflowers of our woods find congenial surroundings.

The many suitable bulbs can be introduced throughout the garden. Without question they bring the first flowers, weeks before the awakening of other plants. Once established, each spring brings forth added beauty. Favorites are the so-called Specie Crocus or Winter-flowering Crocus. Smaller and more refined than the familiar Dutch types, they fit in everywhere to supply masses of early blossom, in shades of cream, yellow, lavender, blue and warm purple. The grassy foliage comes after the flowers, and must be allowed to grow for the next year's harvest. Usually it can be pulled away by late June or early July. Violas, or some other short-lived plant, can fill the bare spot for the rest of the summer.

What other type of garden can bring together in one spot so much beauty and interest? Rock gardening becomes a continuing challenge and obsession for those who love it. It is recommended to all who wish to pursue a stimulating and rewarding hobby.

> 'TO TRAVEL IN THE PLANT KINGDOM YOU SHOULD KNOW THE LANGUAGE.
> IT IS A LIVING LANGUAGE, WITH A PRECISE GRAMMAR, FILLED WITH OVERTONES OF MEANING, INTIMATELY INFLECTED.
> IT HAS, IF YOU LISTEN FOR IT, A LOVELY FALL UPON THE EAR.'
>
> *Donald Culross Peattie*, in THE FLOWERING EARTH

References:

In 1928 and following year 1929 two splendid books on rock gardening were published by Doubleday, Doran & Co., Garden City, N. Y. The author was the informed and distinguished Louise Beebe Wilder. The charm of her writing and the store of information she presented inspired everyone interested in the subject. *Pleasures and Problems of a Rock Garden* and also *Adventures in My Garden and Rock Garden* are as fresh and inspiring to read today as they were over thirty years ago. They have both had a second printing.

Two volumes that have been termed 'the rock gardeners' bible' — *The English Rock Garden*, by Reginald Farrer; a later work, *The Present Day Rock Garden*, by Sampson Clay — contain all the knowledge necessary to the subject. Numerous books helpful to rock gardeners have been published in England and elsewhere. Some are out of print, and can only be had from second-hand book dealers. One of the best is by T. C. Mansfield, titled *Alpines in Colour and Cultivation;* it is well worth seeking out.

Correct pronunciation of botanical names is a rewarding study; formerly, dictionaries gave only genus and species preference, leaving one to guess the pronunciation of varieties. The horticulturist who has *Hortus Second*, Macmillan, 1960, in his library will never be at a loss. The great Liberty Bailey brought out *Hortus First* in 1930, but it is this later work we have needed for so long. To one familiar with plant names, there is an almost musical rhythm in saying them. It is somewhat surprising to find how often the emphasis is on the penult, or the last syllable but one in the word. Regardless of locality, Anglicized pronunciation is the only correct usage.

Unusual Iris for the Rock Garden

William Augustus Peirce
Kittery, Maine

SOME years back, I can remember reading, in *Pleasures and Problems of a Rock Garden*, Mrs. Beebe Wilder's description of her four favorite miniature Iris species: how it had taken her a long time to obtain them: and how, once having done this, she was at last rewarded by seeing them bloom in her garden.

I should like to discuss my own experiences with these — and a few others — in southern Maine.

Iris Arenarius (4") belongs, I believe to the *Regelia* section which requires dryness at certain times of the year. It is the most difficult of the four, or should I say the least permanent. Its common name, Sand Iris, provides one key — which is practically a must to its successful culture. It has diminutive, delicate yellow blossoms somewhat similar in shape to those of the various pumila hybrids. Its own hybrid, "keepsake," in itself attractive, is somewhat taller and coarser than the type, and thoroughly tractable in ordinary soil. It is very effective when planted with the greenish white pumila hybrid, "bridegroom."

Iris Ruthenica (6") has thick grassy foliage and is best described as a refined *Iris Graminea*, except that the color is a clear dark blue and the proportion of flower to fan greater than in the former. It is a *spuria* and easy to grow hereabouts, given adequate moisture. Like many Iris, however, its blooms are evanescent, lasting only for two or three days. There is a dwarf variety, *minor*, also hardy here, which I have not seen.

Iris Gracilipes (7") from Japan, comes in lilac, white, and double lilac, the white form being to my mind the most attractive.

The flowers are flat and about an inch in diameter, exactly like a miniature "Japanese" Iris. It makes a symmetrical tuft up to about ten inches in diameter from which often as many as thirty or forty blooms branch out diagonally like a sunburst.

This Iris should have winter protection in southern Maine as it is reputed to be slightly tender. Division every two or three years is a must (as is the case also with Japanese Iris).

Iris Minuta (5") is the gem of the lot, but clumps require three or four years after transplanting to bloom freely.

The flowers, therefore, which are quite fleeting, are indescribably dainty, sulphur yellow with brown veinings and only about the size of a dime. It does best in some shade and one nursery man recommends lime. The species is perfectly hardy with me and easy to grow with minimum care. I believe Mrs. Wilder claimed it was found only in cultivation (in Japanese gardens), which if true would seem to provide a parallel to the case of the silkworm in the Orient.

There are numerous other dwarf Irises worth growing, not the least attractive among which are some of our own natives. Of these, the best known is *Iris Cristata* (4") which has several forms, some of them tender north and some differing in ease of culture and growth habit, but others easy to keep and increase. These include besides the common lavender blue one, a blue and gold form, a very pale lavender form, dark blues, and an exquiste white variety. There is also a hybrid with *Iris Tectorum, Oliver Twist*, similar to but larger than *Cristata*.

The very dwarf *Iris Lacustris*, found near the Great Lakes, is like a diminutive *Cristata* and is a treasure when it can be procured.

Iris Verna is hardy but difficult, for me, at least. It is a beautiful soft pearly blue with gold on the haft, very low growing and requires shade, moisture and very acid leaf mold.

41

The Western Iris do not do at all well here except for one, *Missouriensis*, which dies back to ground level in the fall. There is a very graceful white variety.

Some of the dwarf bulbous Irises, said to require lime, are very attractive but relatively impermanent here. These include *Bakeriana* and *Histrioides* as well as the well-known *Reticulata* forms.

In conclusion, I should like to put in a word for Iris culture from seed which takes a year or more to germinate, but is quite reliable. I have one very unusual pink *spuria* hybrid, for example, therefrom.

Some Unadvertised Plant Introductions
Sarah R. Childs

THE University of New Hampshire is doing interesting and extremely valuable work in plant breeding. Not being commercial, their programs and successes are not advertised. However, we are all profiting from them in our daily lives, in the improved vegetables and fruits that we eat and the ornamental plants that we see in our own and our friends' gardens.

The University is at Durham, New Hampshire, and was established as a result of The Land Grant Act of 1864. It has grown from a small agricultural college to a university of over 3,600 students, the larger number studying the liberal arts, but with a great many majoring in the sciences, agriculture, forestry and horticulture. The Horticultural Department is outstanding and, in addition to teaching, has done exceptionally successful research work in plant breeding. Many of their introductions have been chosen as All American Selections.

Being largely supported by public funds, the University is not allowed to compete with commercial enterprise, so they cannot sell the seeds of their plants. When a new plant selection proves to have qualities that make it an improvement over the standard ones, it is given a number. The seeds of it are then distributed to qualified individuals, other Agricultural Experimental Stations and commercial seed companies to plant in their trial gardens and evaluate against the standard varieties.

After a period of testing, any variety that is considered worthy of introduction is officially named. Its seeds are then turned over to commercial nurseries and seed companies for production and sale to the general public.

In the past ten years the University has developed over forty new vegetables and many shrubs, perennials, fruits and berries.

There are many reasons for constantly trying to produce new varieties. Disease resistance is, of course, a basic requirement. In New Hampshire perennials must be able to withstand our below zero temperatures. Late blooming spring shrubs have the advantage of not having their buds nipped by an unseasonable frost, and early bearing summer plants are safe from the first fall frosts. Plants from Korea, when crossed with our native ones, have proved very successful in producing this hardiness.

Commercial growers and canners have special requirements. For instance, The Beechnut Company wanted a string bean with white seeds for their baby foods. They pack in glass and the brown seeded beans gave an unattractive color to their products. The University of New Hampshire developed "Green Crop" which has white seeds. This is the one that The Beechnut Company used.

Ease in harvesting and attractive color and shape are important to the market gardener. An example of this is the New Hampshire Midget Watermelon. It is small and round and fits conveniently into a refrigerator. From this was developed the Golden Midget which has two added advantages. It has a much tougher rind so it can withstand rougher handling, and it has a "built-in" ripeness indicator. It turns from green to orange when it is ready to be harvested.

Flavor and food value are also taken into consideration. The University of New Hampshire "Double Rich Tomato" has four times as much vitamin C as the average tomato. It is a cross between "Michigan State" and a plant from Peru. It took ten years and a thousand crosses to develop it.

One of the most important changes in shrub breeding is due to the reduced size of most modern house lots. Individual plants, especially dwarf ones, are better adapted to ranch type houses and small or even moderately large suburban lots. Continuous bloom and interesting color variation in foliage help to make limited landscaping more effective. The "Miss Kim" lilac, a University of New Hampshire introduction, is a perfect example of this. It is a shrub type lilac that does not sucker. It is dwarf — at the age of seven years it is only four feet tall — and its leaves turn burgundy in the fall, thereby producing a longer decorative season.

Another of their outstanding lilac introductions is a pink one, the "James Macfarlane." It is also shrub type with no suckers, but larger than the "Miss Kim." It is a late bloomer, which is a great advantage in cold climates and as an extra dividend, frequently blooms again in midsummer.

The Rose Program of the University of New Hampshire is slanted toward both disease resistance and hardiness. The Durham Pillar is a sensational success. It is a climber that is completely hardy and does not have either mildew or black spot, so does not have to be sprayed with fungicides. It also blooms all summer. The California rose breeders are using it, hoping to develop floribundas and hybrid teas that will have its hardiness and disease resistance.

The Granite Series of chrysanthemums is a great boon to anyone living in a cold climate. These chrysanthemums are completely hardy. They are the result of crossing standard chrysanthemums, for color and form, with ones from Korea, for hardiness.

Fruits, berries, trees and even house plants are being constantly improved through some of their other programs.

These few examples give a general idea of the many ways in which the work of the University of New Hampshire has benefited us. Their contributions, so often anonymous, are extensive and continuing. We can look forward to many more of their outstanding plant introductions in the future. Their Department of Horticulture is always willing to give advice and assistance to anyone on gardening problems.

Growing Small Fruits

Edward J. Rasmussen,
University of New Hampshire, Durham, N. H.

THE success in producing fruit in the home garden depends on the selection of the site, the soil, the choice of kinds and varieties of fruit, timely cultural practices, and a real enthusiasm for gardening.

The best sites are those that are elevated above the surrounding area as they are less subject to frost and extreme winter temperatures than low areas. A well drained loam soil of moderate fertility with an abundance of organic matter is preferred. Sandy loam soils are satisfactory if irrigation is available, but clay and poorly drained soils should be avoided. The importance of a well drained, moderately fertile soil and a good site cannot be over-emphasized. All fruits thrive best when exposed to full sunshine, consequently they should not be planted near wood lots or shade trees. Where sod land is to be used, it is advisable to grow a cultivated crop the year prior to planting small fruits.

Barnyard manure, or good compost, and chemical fertilizers are the best way to improve the organic matter and fertility of the soil. Apply about 700 pounds or ⅓ of a load of manure plus 10 to 15 pounds of a 5-8-7 fertilizer to 1000 square feet. Poultry manure may be substituted for barnyard manure at about one half the amount. Manure should not be used on soils where blueberries are to be grown. The manure and/or fertilizer should be turned under and a good seed bed prepared similar to that for a vegetable garden, by thoroughly cultivating the top soil to a depth of 4 or 5 inches.

Buy from a reputable nursery that can provide first grade plants. *Stunted and dried-out plants offered at reduced prices are no bargain.* As soon as the plants are received from the nursery the packages should be opened, the plants separated in the bundles, moistened and heeled in in a shady place until ready to plant.

The kinds of small fruits that can best be grown in Southern Maine and Southeastern New Hampshire are strawberries, raspberries, blackberries, blueberries and grapes. The planting of currants and gooseberries is prohibited by law because they are a host of the white pine blister rust.

Delicious **RASPBERRIES** and **BLACKBERRIES** which are easily grown in the home garden are becoming more and more scarce on the market. Raspberries and blackberries require the same kind of site, soil and cultural practices as do other small fruit. Contrary to the general belief, raspberries do not thrive in low, wet, shady areas. They grow best on moderately fertile loam soils high in organic matter, and in full sunlight. They require adequate moisture, and during dry periods in the summer some irrigation may be necessary.

The two planting systems in common use are the hedgerow and the hill systems. In the hill system the plants are set 3½ to 4 feet apart in rows 6 to 8 feet apart. Six to ten canes are permitted to grow in each hill. Plant as early in the spring as the ground can be fitted. Dig a hole large enough to accommodate the roots of the plant. Set the plants two inches deeper than they grew in the nursery and pack the soil firmly about the roots and water thoroughly. After planting cut off the canes to the ground level and burn them. This will reduce the source of any disease which might live over on the canes.

Raspberry and blackberry canes grow one year, produce fruit the next year and die shortly after fruiting. For this reason it is necessary to have vigorous new canes developing each year. Soon after harvest remove all of the old canes and any weak new ones at ground level. The following spring, while plants are dormant, thin out the canes to 6 to 10 inches apart, and narrow the hedgerow to 16 to 20 inches wide. Only a light cutting back of the tips is necessary. The best fruiting wood is in the upper half of the cane and heavy cutting back will seriously reduce the size of the crop.

Raspberries are classified as to color of berries and the time of year the fruit is harvested.

There are red, yellow, black and purple raspberries. The red raspberry can also be classified as summer bearing and everbearing. The yellow, purple and black raspberries are summer bearing only.

Red raspberries are the most popular. They are excellent for eating fresh, for freezing, canning and for preserves.

The yellow raspberry is more of a novelty and perfectly delicious. Its use is principally as fresh fruit.

Purple raspberries have a place in the home garden. They are highly

45

productive, fair for eating fresh, excellent for sauce and preserves, and because they produce but few suckers they are easily confined to a limited area.

Black raspberries are less hardy to low winter temperatures and more subject to virus diseases than red raspberries, and probably for these reasons are not as popular as the other varieties. Black raspberries do not reproduce by suckers and are propagated mainly by tip-layering and, like the purple raspberry, can be easily confined to a limited area in the garden.

Good blackberries are easily grown and delicious, but spread rapidly and strongly, and should be planted somewhere where they will not interfere with other plantings.

Varieties of raspberries suggested for planting in this area listed in order of ripening:

Red Raspberries		Yellow Raspberries
Summer Bearing	*Everbearing*	Amber
Sunrise	Durham	
Taylor	September	
Latham	Fall Red	
New Hampshire		
Viking		
Milton		
Purple Raspberries	*Black Raspberries*	*Blackberries*
Success	Cumberland	Darrow
Sodus	Bristol	
	Farmer	

STRAWBERRIES are the most satisfactory small fruit to grow in the home garden, and in choosing varieties it is advisable to select kinds that have been found to grow and produce well in this area.

Strawberry varieties can be divided into two groups — summer bearing and everbearing. Here, summer bearing varieties produce fruit from early June for a period of 3 to 4 weeks depending upon the kinds planted. Where a prolonged harvest is desired, the planting of 4 or 5 varieties that ripen in succession is suggested. Everbearing varieties produce fruit from mid-June to frost.

There are two systems of planting strawberries in general use, the matted row and the hill. The matted row system is preferred for summer-bearing varieties. In this system plants are set 2 to 2½ feet apart in the row and the rows 3½ to 4 feet apart. The runners are permitted to grow and spaced 8 to 10 inches apart to form a matted row 18 to 20 inches wide. Excess runners are removed. All blooms are removed the first season.

The hill system is preferred for everbearing varieties. In the hill system the plants are set in a wide row, spaced one foot apart each way. A space of 2 to 2½ feet is left between each 3 to 4 foot wide planting. All runners are removed at 7 to 10 day intervals throughout the growing season, leaving only the mother plant to produce fruit, which it may be allowed to do the first season.

The best time to plant is in early spring as soon as the ground can be fitted. This is usually the first part of May in this area. The depth at which plants are set is important. Be sure to set the plant so that the crown, the place where the roots are attached, is *just level* or only *slightly* below the soil line. The crown will rot if the plant is set too deep, or dry out with too shallow planting.

Strawberry plants need winter protection. The use of a mulch is an effective way to minimize winter injury. Pine needles, marsh hay and straw are good materials to use for mulch. Do not use any material that will become soggy or that packs tightly such as leaves, shredded corn stalks or sorghum. The mulch should be applied 2 to 4 inches deep over the planting before the temperature drops to 20° F — during the first half of November in this area.

In the spring soon after the young leaves start to grow but before they turn yellow, rake the mulch off the plants into the area between the rows. This will help to conserve moisture, keep the berries clean, and if low temperatures are forecast at blossom time, the mulch can be replaced over the plants for protection against frost.

Strawberry varieties in order of ripening:

Summer Bearing		*Everbearing*	
Earlidawn	Robinson	Red Rich	Ozark Beauty
Howard 17	Sparkle	Gem	Geneva — excellent
Catskill			

HIGHBUSH BLUEBERRIES make a nice addition to small fruit planting. They are excellent for eating and the bushes are most effective in ornamental plantings. By choosing a few varieties that ripen in succession, fruit can be harvested from August to September 15 or later.

Blueberries are quite hardy and will withstand winter temperatures of of –20° F. They are less likely to be injured by late spring frosts than other small fruits, but like other small fruits they do better on an elevated site.

Blueberries are more exacting in soil requirements than other small fruits. They thrive best when grown in moderately fertile, sandy loam to loam soils, with a greater acidity, a pH of 4.3 to 4.8. Have the soil tested before planting blueberries. Contact your county agent or agricultural experiment station for information on this service.

Blueberry plants are shallow rooted, consequently any cultivation should be shallow. They do well under a mulch system of soil management, and this method is suggested for the home garden. Apply a mulch of sawdust, shredded bark or wood shaving 2 to 3 inches deep, and over an area 4 to 5 feet in diameter around the plant. Make additional annual applications as necessary to maintain the above amount. *The mulch helps to control weeds, conserve moisture and keep the soil cool.* Oak leaves and pine needles are also satisfactory material to use for mulch.

Since blueberries require only moderately fertile soil, *manure or legume cover crops should not be used in the preparation of the soil or for fertilizing blueberries.*

Early spring is the preferred time to plant blueberries. Plants are set one inch deeper than they grew in the nursery. Be careful not to set the plants too deep. Deeply set plants are severely retarded in growth until a new set of roots develop near the surface. Space the plants 6 feet apart in rows 8 feet apart. Firm the soil around the roots, water thoroughly to settle the soil, and mulch.

Blueberry plants are available as cuttings and as plants up to 5 years of age. A good 2 to 3 year old plant is the most desirable. Such plants come into bearing earlier than younger ones, are easier to transplant and more likely to survive than older bushes.

On newly set plants remove all weak, spindly growth and cut back shoots that have large, round, blossom buds. These newly set plants should not be permitted to set fruit the first year.

The *second year* remove all weak growth, thin out and head back any bearing shoots. Production the second year on a well grown plant should be limited to not more than one pint of fruit.

The *third year* remove the weak growth. Thin out shoots and cut back the remaining wood to limit production and encourage shoot growth for the next year's crop. The blossom buds are the large buds usually located on the upper half of the shoots. The amount of cutting back will depend upon the vigor of the shoots and the number of blossom buds. Usually cutting back about one fourth of the length of the shoot will produce the desired result.

The amount of pruning for *mature plants* will depend upon the vigor of the plant. Sometimes entire old canes are removed. Remove droopy canes that are too close to the ground. Thin out and cut back remaining shoot growth sufficient to obtain the desired crop. Some experience will help to judge the amount of pruning necessary.

The following varieties in order of ripening are suggested for planting here: Earliblue, Blueray, Bluecrop, Berkley, Pemberton and Jersey. Earliblue begins to ripen about July 20 and Jersey begins to ripen in late August, giving a harvest period of at least 6 weeks. At least two varieties should be planted to insure cross-pollination.

GRAPES definitely have a place in the home garden. The season in this area is not very long, and for this reason the selection of the site for the grape planting is most important. Grapes require full sunlight and high temperatures to ripen their fruits. Select a site on a south slope, or plant the vines on the south side of a windbreak or a building. Early ripening varieties should be chosen. Grapes respond favorably to fertilizer, and a bushel of well-rotted manure per plant, applied early in the spring, is one of the best. If manure is not available, a 10-10-10 fertilizer at the rate of ½ to 1 pound per plant is suggested. High yields of grapes depend upon maintaining vigorous vines, and upon heavy annual pruning. *Pruning has a greater effect* on grape production than any other cultural practice.

Grape varieties in order of their ripening:

Black	*Green or White*	*Red*	*Yellow*
Worden	Portland	Delaware	Golden Muscat — late
Van Buren	Niagara		
Fredonia	Ontario		
Kendaia			

Growing Tree Fruits in the Home Garden

Edward J. Rasmussen,
University of New Hampshire, Durham, N. H.

NOW, with dwarf and semi-dwarf forms available, tree fruits are well adapted to the home garden. They will grow on a wide range of soils provided *the soil is well drained.* Tree fruits do not tolerate "wet feet." Trees planted in wet soils are short lived and stunted. Peach trees grow best on sandy loam to loam soils, while apple, pear and plum trees can be grown on soil which is heavier.

The amount of fertilizer to use will depend upon the fertility of the soil, the growth of the trees and the kind of fruit. The amount of terminal growth and color of foliage are good indicators as to the fertilizer requirement of a tree. Light green or yellowish-green foliage and short terminal growth show lack of fertility. Enough fertilizer should be applied to produce good-sized dark green foliage, and a desirable terminal growth depending upon the kind of fruit. Fruit trees respond best to high nitrogen fertilizers. A general rule to follow is to apply annually ½ pound or 1 cup of a nitrogen fertilizer such as ammonium nitrate for each one inch of trunk diameter of the tree, distributed in a band 2 to 3 feet wide around the tree. If a complete fertilizer such as 10-10-10 is used, double the amount. Peach trees under cultivation should receive only about one half these amounts.

Nearly all fruit trees are now available in dwarf or semi-dwarf form, and for the home garden these are recommended. Dwarf trees will start bearing 2 to 3 years after planting. Semi-dwarf trees start bearing 4 to 5 years after planting. The dwarf trees, because of a limited root system, will require staking. Standard size peaches and plums may be used as they are easily kept small by proper pruning, although the dwarfer forms of these varieties will come into bearing earlier.

It is necessary to plant two or more varieties of most pears, peaches, plums and apples to insure the cross-pollination which will set a satisfactory crop of fruit.

Buy one year old, number 1 grade trees, and request that they be delivered as early in the spring as the soil can be prepared — about the middle of April in this area. Do not let the roots of the trees dry out before or during the planting operation. If they cannot be planted at once, unpack the trees and heel them in immediately upon arrival. To heel in the trees, dig a trench about a foot deep and 15 to 18 inches wide, with one side sloping. Place the trees side by side on the sloping side of the trench, cover the roots with moist soil, firmly packed.

If the trees are dwarf or semi-dwarf they should be planted so that the bud union is an inch or two *above* ground, if the trees are standard size trees, the bud union should be an inch *below* the ground level. Dig a hole large enough to accommodate the roots. Prune back the ends of the roots and remove any broken roots or branches. Firm the soil about the roots and water sufficiently to wet the soil thoroughly.

The growing of **PEACHES** in this area is more of a gamble than growing other tree fruits. The blossoms of most varieties of peach are killed at winter temperatures of –12 to –15° F, and the wood severely injured at temperatures of –20°F. However, hardy new varieties have been developed recently, and unless your garden area has a history of low winter temperatures, it is well worth trying to grow this delicious fruit. Nectarines and apricots will succeed wherever peaches can be grown. Varieties should be chosen for hardiness, and for the season at which they ripen. Fruit may be had over a long period if several varieties which ripen in succession are selected.

PLUMS are an ideal tree fruit for the home garden as they are small in size, come into bearing early and most varieties are hardy to this area. Care should be taken not to over-fertilize, since over-vigorous trees are less productive and are delayed in coming into bearing. European varieties cross-pollinate, and Oriental varieties cross-pollinate each other.

PEARS are the easiest of the tree fruits for the home gardener to grow. They grow on a wide range of soils but do best on heavy soil. Manure should not be used on pears as they respond best to a nitrogen fertilizer applied early in the spring. Most home-grown pears are harvested too late for best quality. They should be picked in a slightly green stage and allowed to ripen in a cool, damp, dark place. Pears ripened on the tree become soft and brown around the core and are poor in quality and flavor. Change in basic color and the ease of separation of the fruit from the tree are two ways that can determine when to pick the fruit. Change in basic color can best be observed on the side of the fruit facing the inside of the tree. The change in color of the skin of the fruit from green to a whitish-green or yellowish-green indicate the best picking time. Do *not* let the fruit become yellow on the tree. Fruit that separates easily from the tree by an upward lift is a fair indication of maturity. If the fruit starts to drop, it has become too ripe. Not all of the stored fruit will ripen at the same time — it should be examined at 5 to 6 day intervals and the ripe fruit sorted out.

Because effective pruning depends so largely on the location and condition of the tree or plant and the purpose for which it is grown, no directions have been given here. Many excellent and well-illustrated books have been written on the subject which can be easily understood, and with a little practice this art may be very quickly acquired.

No instructions for pest control have been included because conditions and materials are so variable. For the best results it is suggested that the reader contact the University of New Hampshire at Durham, N. H., or the University of Maine, at Orono, Maine, for advice about his particular problem.

SOME FRUIT VARITIES IN ORDER OF RIPENING

APPLE
Red Astrachan
Lodi — an improved
   Yellow Transparent
Melba
Duchess
Ottawa 441
Early McIntosh
Puritan
McIntosh
Cortland
Red Delicious
Yellow Delicious
Gilliflower

PEACH
Sunrise
Earlired
Jerseyland
Oriole
Raritan Rose
Golden Jubilee
Red Haven
Cumberland
Colora

NECTARINE
Rivers Orange
New York 884

APRICOT
Early Golden
Moorpark

PEAR
Clapp's Favorite
Bartlett
Gorham
Beurre Bosc
Seckel

PLUM
European
   Stanley Prune
      self-fruitful
   Bradshaw
      self-unfruitful
   Reine Claude
      self-unfruitful
   Yellow Egg
      self-fruitful

Oriental
   Abundance
      self-unfruitful
   Burbank
      self-unfruitful

   Shiro
      self-unfruitful

A Special Peach Tree

Katherine E. Seabury

M Y special peach tree was planted by my own hands, and watched with tender maternal care as each leaf appeared and as it grew taller and taller each year.

During the years, the ground around the trunk of the tree was cultivated until I was exhausted, not a single caterpillar was allowed to wiggle up to its branches, and as Rachel Carson had not yet written her book *Silent Spring*, the tree was sprayed regularly and kept in the utmost robust condition. A few years later my joy overflowed when magnificent rosy peaches appeared on every branch, and my constant care and attention were rewarded.

More years passed, and then my heart was almost broken when I saw fewer and fewer peaches on the tree each summer, and those that did ripen were small and withered.

I went to a seed store, and found a most sympathetic store keeper, who listened to my story with great interest. He recommended some white powder to *feed* my peach tree, and he told me how to do it. The name of the powder was "Agrico," and it is composed of nitrogen, acid, and potash. I shall always think of it with gratitude.

I bought quantities of it, and the gardener and I made a circle of holes around the tree, about six or eight feet away from the trunk. I followed the gardener and filled up the holes he had made, with the magical powder. I hoped that the dampness of the soil would soon melt it, so it would penetrate the earth quickly, and then run off to feed the hungry wandering roots.

It seemed a long time to wait for another summer to see the results of our work, but when it finally arrived, to my delight my special peach tree was again all abloom with gorgeous blossoms, and I watched breathlessly as each blossom turned into a large lucious peach. They all looked like roses among the leaves.

In the fall the tree man told me that I must cut off *two feet* of all the beautiful new branches! I was horrified. I could not believe it. Those waving willowy branches that I loved to watch as they spread out to make the tree taller and added to its perfect symmetry. Of course I had heard all my life that plants and trees had to be pruned, but I never imagined that it meant the brutal amputation of all the young tender branches.

However, in my heart, I was sure the tree man knew more about peach trees than I did, so I shut my eyes and gave the order for the heroic treatment.

In New York one winter, with my peach tree always in my mind, I went to a lecture by Mr. Everett of the New York Botanical Garden. He was to talk on "Fruit Trees," just what I wanted to hear. He was a delightful speaker and the room was filled with ardent Garden Club members.

When Mr. Everett finished his talk, he asked if there were any questions from the audience. There seemed to be none, so I summoned up my courage and asked, "What is the average life of a peach tree?" I had had several worries about my peach tree growing old, and I dreaded the time when it could no longer be my pride and joy.

Mr. Everett answered, "The average life of a peach tree is twenty years," and as the question seemed to stimulate a new line of thought for him, he went on to discuss the ways and means to keep large orchards alive, with drainage, cultivation and stimulation.

He addressed these remarks chiefly to me, as I had been the one to bring up the subject of peach trees. But while he was talking, I was terrified lest he should ask me suddenly, "How large is your orchard?" And I, timid but truthful, would have to reply, "I have only one peach tree."

Strawberries on the Front Porch

Ruth Metcalf

I was charmed by the beautiful strawberry plants at the Flower Show in March, so selected four of the climbing variety Sonjana. We left them in the small florists pots in an east window where they flourished until May. By then they were too large and called for a little ingenuity. A pair of fair sized redwood tubs one foot square, previously used for geraniums, were filled with my good potting soil with 2 handfuls of bovung sprinkled around the edge away from the plants. The tubs were put in the same east window and soon were covered with handsome foliage and began to put out runners.

About the first of June we moved them outside to each side of our doorstep with its nice sunny exposure to the south. A four foot tomato stake anchored in the tubs with bricks served as a path for the runners which soon were covered with blossoms.

By July 1st we began to get strawberries and believe it or not, continued to do so until we had a frost in October. They remained covered with green leaves long after the other foliage had begun to turn. Many were the comments received. "Are those Strawberries?" "I thought Strawberries grew on the ground in fields." Perhaps the best was from a neighbor's 12-year-old boy, "Gee, these are great, after you ring the bell you can eat strawberries while you wait."

Growing Directions: Place them in a sunny location and water freely each day preferably in the evening. After repotting put them back in the same location for at least a week — they will do much better. My mixture for potting soil; in a bushel basket mix well together

> 2 spadefuls of loam
> 1 spadeful of sand
> 1 spadeful of compost
> 1 3 in. flower pot of bovung
> 1 3 in. flower pot of lime stone
> 2 3 in. flower pots of bone meal.

Espalier Work Is Creative

Sidney F. Bohlen

OF all forms of gardening none offers a wider scope for following your own ideas than the espalier. Starting from what resembles a twig you keep your strongest side shoots at regular intervals — and after that you are on your own. We started ours after my husband had finally become interested in doing useful things about the place. He said, "I'm going to make two arms into an arch and meet in the middle." Anything rather than dampen his ardor, I said "go ahead." The results have been sensational — television, evergreen book and much publicity. Dubious as I was, the ugly blank wall is now an arresting sight.

Whatever material is used start by cutting back all but one or two straight branches. Allow these to grow about three feet tall, then pick your strongest and best placed side shoots for your design and cut away all others right down to the trunk of the branch. As you continue pruning leave a bit of new growth, rubbing out all side shoots not necessary to your great plan.

Espaliers were started abroad as a matter of thrift. The small plot of land around the little cottage was much too precious to waste on shade-producing branches. They grew all manner of fruit against the wall with the dual purpose of covering bareness and having room for vegetables and the adorable little flower gardens. The fruit ripened earlier against a sunny wall protected from the wind. In our country we use them as a decorative piece for a place that needs covering, walls, places between windows or chimneys.

We glue bendable wire attachments (Wayward Vine Guide & Support) to the wall, securely holding the branch until strong enough to stand alone. Wire and wooden frames can also be used. Many flat designs may be invented. The usual ones are fan, candelabra, U-shaped or simplest of all just vertical arms. The main stem on a corner with arms going on opposite walls is unusual. Eastern exposure is best as midday sun can overheat where wires are used as a foundation.

On a wooden wall it is best to build a frame of your design to prevent rotting the foundation wall. The exposure depends a good deal on the material but our best results have been northeastern. The midday sun can be too hot against a wall but this rarely happens north of the Merrimack. The following can easily be trained for espalier work: Forsythia, Pyracantha, Cotoneaster, flowering dogwood in a protected spot, yew, and all fruits.

The only requisite is to be a ruthless pruner — hence the choice of tough material is advisable. After the design has been established continual pinching out and cutting off new shoots that are detrimental to your pattern will keep it symmetrical and in order.

Your work is never done but it is fun. The constant care makes you feel that your plant is a member of the family.

Espaliered Fruit Trees

Marion P. Hosmer

THE most unusual, beautiful and rewarding experiment in our garden by the sea is the fruit trees espaliered on the walls of the house which is of native stone. The house faces south toward the sea, and apples trained into fan shape, and U-shaped pear trees fill the spaces between the door and windows of the south wall. On the east side is another apple, while the sunnier west end supports a peach and an enormous plum.

We planted all of these trees ten years ago, as soon as the house was built and before the terrace on the south front was laid. When we purchased them from Henry Leuthardt, Port Chester, New York, the trees were five years old and already shaped. They came beautifully crated, and we hardly had them in the ground that first spring, before the apples were in bloom. They bore a few apples that year. The other fruits took longer to bloom and bear.

When in Europe one sees houses with the entire walls covered with espaliered fruit trees, one imagines that this is the result of many years of growth. However, after only ten years all of our trees are two storeys tall, and completely cover the wall. They are beautiful all the year, with the warm brown branches, crimson twigs and fat buds in the winter, the fragrant spring bloom, and in the fall, the fruit hanging like jewels against the grey stone. We often pick a bushel of apples from one tree, and there are more plums than we can eat. The peach and pears are not quite so prolific.

As our walls are of stone, the trees can be fastened directly to them. The best nail is the English wall nail which can be driven into cracks, or into the mortar, and to which the branches are tied — preferably with narrow strips of rawhide which is soft and will stretch, and so not cut into the tree. Even with this, the ties should be checked several times a season to avoid girdling the branches. On wooden houses it is best to build a lattice a few inches away from the wall to support the trees, which may be tied directly to it. The lattice may be hinged at the bottom, so that when painting is necessary, lattice and tree may be gently leaned forward a few degrees to allow access to the wall.

These trees, confined as they are between wall and terrace, need to be heavily fed, and we do so, with bone meal fall and spring, and a good general fertilizer two or three times during the summer. The spray program is slightly different than that for the orchard trees, as the warmth of the wall brings the espaliered ones into leaf and bloom before those in the open field. For this reason we spray them with the same general-purpose spray, and at the same time, as the roses that grow in the terrace garden. The only exception is that the fruit trees are not sprayed while they are in bloom. This would destroy the insects that are busy pollinating the blossoms.

Pruning is the trickiest job of all, and must be done spring and fall and each month during the summer. Until the trees are well established, pruning should be light and designed to keep the trees well-shaped. For apples, pears, and plums, prune side shoots to eight inches and forward growing shoots to four inches. Peaches present another problem, as they only bear fruit on the new wood. It might be best to consult a book with diagrams before tackling them. All of these trees will bear heavily once established and correctly pruned. The fruit should be thinned (also a form of pruning), both to produce large fruit and to lighten the load on the tree so that it will not pull away from its supports, nor be weakened from too heavy bearing.

Once you understand the growing habits of each tree and how it should be pruned, you can train your own espaliers from young whips of trees. Walks or gardens may be fenced with upright or horizontal (cordon) espaliers, or a summer house may be created from fruit trees trained on a wood or metal frame. Here one may sit and delight in the blossoms and fruit of these most amenable of trees.

Bibliography:

Plant Pruning in Pictures, Montague Free, Doubleday and Co.

The Pruning Book, L. H. Bailey, The Macmillan Co.

Trained and Sculptured Plants, A Handbook, Brooklyn Botanic Garden.

Pruning Handbook, Brooklyn Botanic Garden.

The Short Season Vegetable Garden

Roland E. Roberts,
University of Maine, Orono, Maine

VEGETABLE gardening in Maine offers a unique challenge to the creative person, for gardening is an art. Armed with some scientific background and experience with the tools and techniques of gardening a person can express creative ability as do others with various art forms. Apart from the relaxing nature of creative gardening other satisfactions are realized. To serve summer guests with salads of supreme quality or piping hot sweet corn dipped in butter produced in one's own garden is a very tangible personal reward for many gardeners.

Our friends who summer in Maine do so to experience the comfortably cool nights and mildly warm days of our summer. When they go about their gardening they are confronted with this same climate which is not always cooperative. Like it or not, most vegetables prefer a warmer climate than is found in any part of Maine.

It is the aim of nearly every vegetable gardener to harvest vegetables as early in the season as possible. Others of us derive our satisfaction from having a truly productive garden where the plants are vigorous and healthy so that a bountiful harvest is assured. Countless others till for the love of tilling and plant a garden mainly for the sheer joy of watching plants as they grow and develop.

LOCATION

Regardless of the motives for gardening the guidelines for success are the same. Since we can not improve the climate in outdoor gardens our practices must be tailored to derive best use of the resources at our disposal.

To capture the greatest possible amount of heat from the sun your vegetable garden must be out in the open where it can get at least six hours of direct sunlight, unobstructed by trees or the home. Your garden soil must provide the chemical compounds, including water, which are necessary for productive growth. Soil texture, which is the term used to describe the relative proportion of sand and clay comprising a soil, governs the productive potential of your garden. You may be fortunate enough to have a deep, sandy loam. If you have no choice but to locate your garden on clay be ready to incorporate extra organic materials such as sawdust, or peat that is already partially decomposed. Sandy loam soil is desirable because it is usually well drained and for this reason is warmer than clay

57

soils in the early part of the growing season. Early soils are of utmost importance in Maine where every degree of heat counts. An area with a southern exposure is the best possible position for an early vegetable garden.

For a short season garden vegetables should be selected for their ability to grow and develop in a relatively short period. The first concern of most gardeners is to have vegetables to fashion a salad. Lettuce of the leaf and butterhead types, cucumbers, radishes, tomatoes, carrots and cabbage do very well in this category. Weather can raise havoc with head lettuce, so it is a poor risk in a small, short-season garden. Several vegetables which are usually cooked before serving and easy to grow are snap beans, yellow and green summer squash, beet greens, chard and sweet corn. Unless fast-maturing sweet corn varieties are chosen, results with this crop may be disappointing.

Kinds and varieties of vegetables that will grow well in Maine are listed in Table 1. Plant breeders have developed these outstanding vegetable varieties in cooperation with specialists in human nutrition and taste testing. The suggested varieties have been fully tested under Maine growing conditions by the Plant and Soil Sciences Department of the University of Maine and have shown potential for this area. No single vegetable variety resists all disease organisms that may attack it. Disease resistant varieties are recommended whenever their availability is established.

Figure 1 outlines a planting arrangement for a small garden. Since there is no "right" plan for all gardens this one is intended simply as a model to serve as a guide in developing a plan which will reflect your individual desires and preferences.

SOIL FERTILITY

Proper Management of Lime, Fertilizers and Manure

The mineral soils of the northeast are naturally very acid. Some of the soils in this region have desirable texture, but they are not naturally fertile in the nutrients required by vegetables. However, by wise management of limestone and a complete fertilizer the fertility of this soil can be raised to a point that is close to optimum. Nearly all vegetables grow best in soil that is just slightly acid — the pH being about 6.5. At this level of acidity, nutrients can be made available to the plants in balanced proportions with the result that the vegetables will be productive and of high quality.

Fertilization of vegetable garden soils by "guesstimation" is like playing Russian Roulette — it's a hit or miss game, and the risk is high. A wrong guess in garden fertilization is bound to result in disappointment. The best method to use in determining lime and fertilizer requirements for a garden soil is to submit samples to a reliable soil testing service for analysis. Land grant colleges of life sciences and agriculture in the northeast test soil and offer lime and fertilizer recommendations to aid gardeners who wish to improve the fertility of their garden soils.

Very often an application of one hundred to two hundred pounds of limestone per one thousand square feet of garden soil is required to raise the pH to the optimum range. The fertilizer grades best suited to home vegetable gardening are 5-20-10 and 5-10-10. Many other ratios of nitrogen, phosphorus, and potassium are available, but the 1-4-2 and the 1-2-2 are best for the majority of cases. An initial broadcast application of three to five pounds of 5-20-10 is usually required before planting. Gardeners will find it helpful to stock a fertilizer containing only nitrogen. Nitrogen fertilizer is used as a sidedressing for vegetables like sweet corn, cucumbers and tomatoes. These are some of the vegetables that usually respond to additional nitrogen applied about half way through the growing season. On small areas about one pound of ammonium nitrate (33% actual nitrogen) or three quarters of a pound of urea (45 percent actual nitrogen) per one hundred linear feet of row is a usual application. The nitrogen fertilizer should be applied in a band near the row but not on the plants since it will scorch the leaves.

Limestone and fertilizer that is applied before sowing seeds or setting plants must be thoroughly mixed into the upper six inches of top soil. Otherwise root burning may result or the limestone may not be distributed evenly enough to be of any benefit.

Reference:

Vegetable Varieties for Maine, Pamphlet 87, Cooperative Extension Service, University of Maine, Orono, Maine.

TABLE 1. Varieties, Space, Seed and other suggestions for A Short Season Vegetable Garden in Maine.

Vegetable Varieties	Yield per 100 Feet of Row Approximate	Seed or Plants per 100 Feet of Row	Earliest Planting Time	Depth of Planting	(Hand Cultivated) Approximate Distance Between	
					Rows	Plants
Asparagus:						
Waltham Washington*	50 lbs.	1 oz. or 75 plants	April 15	1 in.	2 ft.	18 in.
Beans:						
Green Snap-Contender*, Stringless Black Valentine	30 lbs.	½ lb.	May 25	1 in.	3 ft.	3 in.
Wax — Eastern Butterwax*	30 lbs.	½ lb.	May 25	same	same	same
Lima — Thaxter*, Nemagreen*	25 lbs. (in pods)	½ lb.	June 1	same	same	4 in.
Beet:						
Early — Crosby Green Top*	70 lbs. (topped)	2 oz. or 400 plants	April 15	½ in.	18 in.	3 in.
Summer — Ruby Queen	40 lbs. of greens	same	same	same	same	same
Broccoli:						
Early — Spartan Early*	50 lbs.	1 pkt or 75 plants	April 15	½ in.	3 ft.	18 in.
Midseason — Calabrese*	same	same	same	same	same	18 in.
Brussels Sprouts: Jade Cross	100 lbs.	1 pkt or 75 plants	April 15	½ in.	3 ft.	18 in.
Cabbage:						
Early — Wisconsin Golden Acre, Babyhead	135 lbs.	1 pkt or 100 plants	April 10	½ in.	3 ft.	12 in.
Midseason — Marion Market, Savoy		1 pkt or 100 plants	same	same	same	same
Red — Red Acre		1 pkt or 100 plants	same	same	same	same

	Yield	Amount to Plant	Planting Date	Depth	Row Spacing	Plant Spacing
Carrot: Nantes*	65 lbs. (topped)	1 packet	May 1	½ in.	18 in.	2 in.
Cauliflower: Early — Snowcap*	125 lbs.	1 pkt or 70 plants	April 15	½ in.	3 ft.	24 in.
Celery: Waltham Summer Pascal	300 lbs.	1 pkt or 200 plants	June 1	⅛ in.	2 ft.	6 in.
Corn, Sweet: 1st Early-Spring Gold, Sugar & Gold*	100 ears	2 oz. or 100 potted plants	May 25	1 to 2 in.	3 ft.	12 in.
2nd Early -Early Sunglow*, Golden Beauty*		same	same	same	same	same
Cucumber (Slicing): Downeast Slicer, Fletcher, or Improved Highmoor Pickling-Wisconsin SMR-18	200 lbs.	1 pkt or 75 potted plants	June 1	¼ in.	6 ft.	3 ft.
		same	same	same	same	same
Dandelion: Improved Thick Leaf*	40 lbs.	1 packet	April 15	½ in.	18 in.	12 in.
Eggplant: Black Magic Hybrid	90 lbs.	1 pkt or 50 plants	June 1	¼ in.	3 ft.	3 ft.
Endive: Broadleaf-Full Heart Batavian	75 heads	1 pkt or 100 plants	April 15	½ in.	18 in.	12 in.
Curled Leaf-Salad King		same	same	same	same	same
Kohlrabi: Early White Vienna Early Purple Vienna	65 lbs.	1 packet	April 15	½ in.	18 inch	6 in.
Kale: Vates	75 lbs.	1 pkt or 50 plants	April 1	1 in.	12 in.	2 ft.

Vegetable Varieties	Yield per 100 Feet of Row Approximate	Seed or Plants per 100 Feet of Row	Earliest Planting Time	Depth of Planting	(Hand Cultivated) Approximate Distance Between Rows	Plants
Lettuce:						
Crisphead — Great Lakes 659	50 heads	1 pkt or 100 plants	April 15	½ in.	18 in.	12 in.
Butterhead — Dark Green Boston Butterhead (Bibb Type) Buttercrunch	80 heads	same	same	same	same	same
Leaf — Grand Rapids, Ruby, Salad Bowl	80 heads	same	same	same	same	same
Cos (Romaine) — Paris Island	90 heads	same	same	same	same	same
Muskmelon: Maincrock Hybrid	100 lbs.	1 pkt or 50 plants	June 1	1 in.	6 ft.	2 ft.
Watermelon: New Hampshire Midget	100 lbs.	1 pkt or 50 plants	June 1	1 in.	6 ft.	2 ft.
New Zealand Spinach (as such)	100 lbs.	1 packet	June 1	1 in.	3 ft.	18 in.
Onion:						
Seeded — Early Harvest	75 lbs.	1 packet	May 1	½ in.	18 in.	3 in.
Plants — Sweet Spanish	100 lbs.	1 pkt or 300 plants	same	2 in.	same	same
Sets — Ebenezer	75 lbs.	1 lb.	same	1 in.	same	same
Parsnip:						
Early — All-America	70 lbs.	1 packet	May 10	½ in.	18 in.	2 in.
Peas:						
Early — Frosty*, Freezonian*	30 lbs.	½ lb.	May 1	¼ in.	36 in.	1 in.
2nd Early — Lincoln*	40 lbs.	same	same	1 in.	36 in.	same

Pepper:

Sweet, thin wall & Italian Sweet	70 lbs.	1 pkt or 70 plants	June 10	¼ in.	3 ft.	18 in.
Sweet, thick wall — Pennwonder*	100 lbs.	same	same	same	same	same
Hot, long-Cayenne	50 lbs.	same	same	same	same	same
Hot, round-Large Red Cherry	50 lbs.	same	same	same	same	same
Radish:						
Red — Champion	40 bnchs	1 oz.	May 1	½ in.	12 in.	1 in.
White — Icicle		same	same	same	18 in.	same
Rutabaga: Laurentian	100 lbs.	½ oz.	May 10	¼ in.	24 in.	3 in.
Rhubarb: Valentine	100 lbs.	25 plants	May 1	just cover	4 ft.	3 ft.
Spinach: America*	40 lbs.	1 oz.	April 15	½ in.	18 in.	4 in.
Squash: Bush Buttercup	400 lbs.	½ oz. or 30 ptd pls	June 1	1 in.	4 ft.	3 ft.
Summer — Early Prolific Straight Neck	150 lbs.	same	same	same	same	same
Green Summer — Zucchini Hybrid Storrs Green Hybrid	150 lbs.	same	same	same	same	same
Tomato: Fireball, Moreton Hybrid, PXF Hybrid	300 lbs.	1 pkt or 35 to 50 potted plants	June 10	½ in.	3 to 4 ft.	1½ to 3 ft.
Turnip: Yellow Globe	75 lbs.		May 10	¼ in.	18 in.	2 in.

*Indicates varieties well suited for freezing.

63

FIGURE 1.   Planting Arrangement for a Small Vegetable Garden.   (Not to Scale)

Asparagus*   Rhubarb*   Chives*

Planting Succession	Row # and Width		Asparagus*		Rhubarb* (30 ft.)	Chives*
	1 – 3'		1st Early sweet corn		2nd Early sweet corn	......
	2 – 3'		1st Early sweet corn		2nd Early sweet corn	......
	3 – 3'		1st Early sweet corn		2nd Early sweet corn	......
3rd	4 – 3'		Fireball tomato (on ground)		PX or Moreton Hybrid on trellis	......
	5 – 3'	Celery	Peppers		Eggplant	......
	6 – 4'		Summer squash (½ green & ½ yellow)		Bush Buttercup	......
	7 – 6'		Muskmelon		Watermelon	......
	8 – 6'		Slicing Cucumbers		Pickling Cucumbers	......
2nd	9 – 3'		Green snap beans		Wax snap beans	......
	10 – 3'	Lima beans				
	11 – 1½'	Carrots				
	12 – 1½'		Parsnips		Radishes (several plantings)	......
	13 – 1½'	Spinach	Beets		Swiss Chard	......
	14 – 1½'	Ruby lettuce	Salad Bowl lettuce		Buttercrunch lettuce	......
	15 – 1½'	Endive	Buttercrunch lettuce		Grand Rapids lettuce	......
1st	16 – 3'		Golden Acre cabbage		Marion Market cabbage	......
	17 – 3'	Kale	Red Acre cabbage		Kohlrabi	......
	18 – 3'		Spartan Early broccoli		Calabrese broccoli	......
	19 – 3'		Cauliflower			......
	20 – 3'		Early onions		Brussels sprouts	......
	21 – 2'		Rutabaga or Turnip		Late onions (from seed)	......
4th	22 – 3'		Miscellaneous later plantings of certain			
	23 – 3'		fast growing kinds			
	24		Expansion area for odds and ends			

*Perennial and biennial crops which remain year after year.

Part of the garden should be planted to a soil-improving grass crop each year. Even in a small garden the practice of crop rotation is essential to continued productivity.

64

Broadminded About Broad Beans

Muriel Howells

ENGLAND, Ireland and Portugal are only three of the countries which grow, eat, and appreciate the Broad Bean. Why aren't we more broad-minded about them here in the United States?

These beans are slightly larger than lima beans and have an interesting, if perhaps acquired, taste all their own. My husband grew up loving them and I have noticed that our children always seem to take their vacations during Broad Bean time and they have admonished us to wait until they are home again before we deplete our frozen supply.

For his garden in southern Maine, my father-in-law used to buy the seeds in the early spring at the local seed store where they were called English Broad Beans. Now, in these days of Progress, we can no longer buy the seeds here and although some larger seed distributors sometimes sell them as Fava beans, they often run short of them. So every February my husband writes to the United States Department of Agriculture in Hoboken, N. J., saying that he wants to get the seed in England. He asks for the appropriate labels and certificates which arrive very promptly. These he sends straight to Sutton and Sons, Reading, England, with his order. Sutton lets him know how much they are and happily takes his check drawn on a U. S. bank.

Sutton lists nine varieties of "White-Seeded" Broad Beans and five varieties of "Green-Seeded." When the pods are shelled, the bean has an inner coat or skin, grayish white with green meat in the former, and green skin with bright green meat in the latter. We do not bother to peel the skin before cooking, although the bean is more tender if you do. After many thoughtful meals, we have decided that "Unrivalled Green Windsor" is our favorite. This has seven to nine beans in a long pod.

The seeds arrive with directions for planting in "February," but, don't forget, this refers to England. For *New* England, they should be planted after the last frost which we interpret, here near the water, as April 20th. They should be planted about four inches deep, in good garden loam, with plenty of manure, compost or other fertilizer, and in double rows, allow-ing six to nine inches between the two lines forming the rows, with two to three feet *between* the rows.

By June 1st, they are three inches high, and start to blossom on the 15th. They grow on a large upright stalk, entirely different from any other beans. About June 25th, we pinch off the main top stalk, leaving three or four stems of blossoms so they will grow plenty of beans but will only grow three or four feet in height, and not so tall that they would need support. Occasionally a few aphids appear in the top tender buds and are promptly sprayed with nicotine sulphate or isotex. The pods start to form nicely by the end of June and we eat them happily from the 20th of July to the 15th of August.

The blossoms are white and black like a coarse, but chic, sweet pea. This causes a special hazard to our crop, as I am apt to dismay my husband by prematurely cutting an armful for a flower arrangement.

However, the surviving beans are devoured with delight and some beans are always saved to be carefully frozen. They freeze well and it is a simple process: Put the beans, in their pods, in boiling water for four minutes; cool in cold water, shell; pack tightly in polyethylene bags, tie, wrap in freezer paper, seal, mark, and freeze. When they are cooked eight to ten minutes in boiling, salted water, I doubt if anyone could tell the difference between the frozen and the fresh.

If we are lucky enough to have a handful of cooked beans left over, I put them in the blender with beef or chicken stock and seasoning, and heat it later with perhaps a dash of milk or cream and strain it to make a wonderful, and subtle, soup.

The Broad Bean's yield is great in proportion to the land it uses and it has a long harvest season. In short, this bean has a lot to offer and we love it — we may sound prejudiced, and we are. If you want a different opinion, just ask my mother!

Rebuilding an Overgrown Garden
Constance H. Stanley

WHEN we bought our Victorian house, *circa* 1883, overlooking the sea in southern Maine, we did so against the advice of our relatives and city friends and even the real estate man through whom we acquired it. We knew the house was not all one could wish for, architecturally, but somehow, to us the property held an irresistible charm. We also knew we were acquiring a major gardening and landscaping problem. The place had been unoccupied for five or six years which meant sadly neglected grounds and gardens. Nature had been hard at work, however, and the result was a horticultural nightmare.

But far from being discouraged, we regarded this situation as a challenge which we thought would be fun to accept. The jungle that had taken over was our first point of attack which meant cutting down, thinning out, up-rooting and, in general, restoring some semblance of order where chaos existed. It was a big and strenuous undertaking for us because much·

of the work we had to do ourselves. Yet the chore has been amply rewarding. Already we can see the fruits of our efforts taking shape, even though we have been at it for only two short years.

We had three different areas to reclaim — the public area at the front of the house, where there is adequate space for parking several cars in the driveway — the service, or delivery area, with its walk directly to the kitchen door, well screened from the front of the house — and the family or private area at the back of the house which provides an ocean view.

The public area, or front driveway, presented a real problem. We sought advice from local nurserymen and two of our garden club acquaintances. The entrance drive from the street to the circular parking area brings into the view of the visitor, as he enters, the garden at the front of the house. Originally there was no garden there at all, merely a tumbled-down stonewall at the bottom of a slope about thirty feet beyond the far edge of the circular drive. First, we rebuilt the section of old stonewall that was visible from the drive. At the left end of the new wall we provided an opening and path which led to a field spotted with white birches, giving a pleasing vista and a feeling of depth. On either side of this opening we planted Alberta Spruce. All the planting in front of the wall, which is rather low, is dwarfed — a sprawling Mugho Pine occupies the center. Taxus, Daphne and Yellow-Flowering Azaleas surround this main focal point. Many Yellow Double-Tulip bulbs were put in last fall and this spring we shall add clumps of Lily of the Valley along the base of the wall.

At the service entrance we put in a garden where none had been before. This was a family project which produced startling results as well as fun. We all had a hand in clearing this semi-circular spot and planting it with a profusion of annuals in eye-catching colors. When in bloom the results were amazing. Basically it was simply what might best be called an old-fashioned garden. In the front were Yellow and White Pansies and Pink and Blue Sweet-Alyssum — then came Pink Zinnias, Lemon-Yellow Marigolds, Blue Phlox, Bright Red, Old Fashioned Pinks and Verbenas in pink and red. Above, in back, were rows of tall, Blue Batchelor Buttons, Snap Dragons and *Nicotiana affinis* in white, pink, yellow and deep red. The terrain of this garden is a gentle slope that rises from our lane towards the east side of the house and in back of the garden is a wonderful, big ledge which we have cleared of vines, blackberry briers and assorted weeds. Eventually it should make a delightful rock garden and it has already a respectable start. A pretty, old apple tree spreads its graceful branches over the ledge.

The private or family area has been a major reclamation project. Here the jungle was at its worst. Where once had been flower-bordered walks, groupings of Day Lilies, Iris and Roses, grew black alder, briers, bayberry, wild raspberry, juniper, and even poison ivy. As yet we have done little planting here. The work of cutting out unwanted growth, trimming salvageable shrubs and pruning trees, cleaning out old flower beds, digging up roots and reseeding large areas with grass and clover required all our available time during the past summer and fall.

This area, some three-quarters of an acre in size, slopes rather sharply away from the back of the house. At the far edge is a fine, flat-faced stonewall, covered here and there with overhanging ivy. In back of the wall old lilac bushes provide the means for wisteria vines to climb and flower in the spring. Beyond, on a clear day, the sparkling ocean adds its beauty to the view from the veranda on the back of the house. Our work here has just begun but it will be our main project this year and probably for several years to come, from spring to fall. Then we must find some time for watching mother nature take over to add her inimitable touch to what we have prepared for her to work upon.

A Thought When Laying Out a Garden
Nancy Greene

STEADIED by her cane, Miss Llewellyn Parsons stood at one end of the glowing patchwork of flowers which made up her garden. Beyond, the blue ocean stretched to the horizon.

Miss Parsons did not believe in wasting words:

" Walk through your garden towards the sun. This gives brilliance and depth, light and shadow. In the morning I walk through one path. In the afternoon I use another facing West, always toward the sun. A garden should be planned this way."

The tide was low. Seals lay on the rocks basking in the lazy heat. Seabirds floated on the waves. It was Miss Parsons' kingdom.

The August Doldrums,
Their Prevention and Cure
Sarah R. Childs

HOW often have we heard, "There's *nothing* blooming in my garden in August."

August does produce a gardening problem. The spring perennials have gone by, the fall ones are not even showing color, the annuals that were so effective during July are leggy and spent, and the roses are between bloomings.

From the discouragement and disappointment of many years I have gradually found the following preventions and cures:

The ideal solution is to buy flats of annuals just coming into bloom, but that is seldom possible. Any annuals still left in the nurseries are usually in worse shape than those in the garden.

Many perennials can be transplanted in bloom — phlox, early chrysanthemums and physostegia are some of the commonest. Even if these aren't necessarily the plants that we want permanently or take up space that is needed for the annuals, they make good temporary replacements and can be saved to use again another year if there is a place where they can be wintered — such as a cutting garden.

Potted plants from the greenhouses are more expensive but very effective. Chrysanthemums, browallia, geraniums and tuberous begonias are all good.

A very small seed bed, planted in early June, can produce quantities of annuals ready to be transplanted into the borders in August. Sweet alyssum, candytuft, ageratum, marigolds, zinnias, bachelor buttons, salvia and nicotiana are some of the most satisfactory.

Another use for a seed bed is for planting extra flats, bought in June, of petunias, pansies, snapdragon, etc. Keep them cut back until the middle of July. In August they will be shapely and in bloom and can be exchanged for the spent ones.

Groups of five or seven gladiolus corms can be planted in the borders in late May. I prefer the miniatures but in some places the larger ones are excellent. They take up very little space, have interesting foliage, and their spikes of bloom make an excellent accent.

Many of the lilies bloom in August. These can either be planted permanently or potted and moved into the garden when in bloom.

Peruvian daffodils (Ismene) are extremely effective. They bloom within two or three weeks after planting and can be kept in a cool cellar until the first part of July. Their blossoms are beautiful and their foliage is striking, amaryllis-like in form and a lovely rich green in color.

I find that by using all, or a combination, of these solutions my garden *does* have a lot of bloom in it in August.

Annuals North of the Merrimack

Edna Roberts and Sarah R. Childs
York, Maine

THE advantages of annuals are many. They require no long range planning, no permanent ownership of land, and no fall, winter or early spring maintenance and care. They provide color in mid-summer when spring and fall perennials are not in bloom. They make an effective display for comparatively little cost and, most important of all, give continuous bloom throughout the summer.

North of the Merrimack River the frost comes late in the spring and early in the fall. Some annuals are more successful here than others, and some need to be treated differently from those grown where the season is longer.

Many can be raised from seed sown directly in the ground either, as noted on the packages "as soon as the soil is warm" or "after all danger of frost is past."

When the soil IS warm the following can be planted and will bloom early in July: alyssum, baby's breath, bachelor buttons, bells of Ireland, calendula, clarkia, cleome, gaillardia, godetia, larkspur, love-in-a-mist, mignonette, nasturtiums, sweet peas, and many herbs.

After all danger of frost is over seeds of these more tender varieties may be planted: candytuft, cosmos, datura, dianthus, Unwin dahlias, marigolds, morning glory, portulaca, blue salvia, scabiosa, statice, strawflowers and zinnias.

Due to the shortness of our season many others must be planted indoors in flats or bought from a grower.

Mrs. Edna Roberts of The Cider Hill Greenhouses in York, Maine, is well known throughout New England for her flats of annuals. Mrs. Roberts says that she specializes in planting flats of only one color and variety to enable her customers to make harmonious plans for their gardens. Drifts of flowers of the same hue are far more attractive than the spotty effect created by mixed colors.

Mrs. Roberts says that she specializes in planting flats of only one color and variety to enable her customers to make harmonious plans for their gardens. Drifts of flowers of the same hue are far more attractive than the spotty effect created by mixed colors.

Also, instead of limiting her flats to include only the old stand-bys such as zinnias, marigolds, petunias, snapdragons, etc., Mrs. Roberts has tried innumerable less common ones. She buys many seeds from England and from lesser known seedsmen in this country who list unusual varieties and colors.

She has had excellent success with ageratum "Little Blue Star", tall ageratum, anagallis, anchusa "Bluebird", yellow asters, yellow carnations, summer chrysanthemums, English dianthus, dimorphotheca (Cape daisy), echium, feverfew "Little Star", pink or blue lace flower, lobelia "Cambridge Blue", giant English mignonette, pink or blue nemesia, lime green nicotiana, nierembergia, torenia, and verbenas in straight colors.

Not all annuals will be killed by the first frosts. Many will continue to bloom until a hard freeze. Snapdragons, pansies, petunias, nicotiana, salvia farinacea, sweet alyssum, stock, carnations, verbena, mignonette and other stalwarts will prove valuable in providing a long season of continuous bloom in the annual garden.

Annuals for Visual Effect

Constance T. Johnson

PLANTING fast-growing, colorful but inexpensive annuals was more or less routine for me during some three decades of marriage to a Naval Officer. We had innumerable homes for periods ranging from three months to six years, here and abroad, in tropical heat and northern cold, with sandy soil, red clay, and infrequently anything rich and dark. Usually we assumed the responsibility of the outside appearances of these *pieds-à-terre.*

Before we bought our present home in York Harbor after my husband's retirement, we rented for the three summer months a house which for some time had been occupied only a few weeks each year in August or September. Here we used the same old system outside to achieve as soon as possible a bright, lived-in appearance.

As of June first the property abounded with many lovely ferns, bushes, and shrubbery, but the one long flowerbed (about 80 feet) across the front lawn was completely enveloped with myriad weeds and vines. A few early perennials struggled to find the sun. Later we discovered some day lilies, thistle and oriental poppies.

Expediency was the word in clearing away the weeds, roots, and rocks. After several days of hard work the edging was delineated and the ground turned and ready for planting. Inasmuch as we were to move out the first of September, we did not bother to add any humus to the soil, use any plant food, or pesticides. We watered regularly, and weeded occasionally.

With the river as a back-drop, and a pleasant open porch about forty feet away, we planted several flats of giant Yellow Globe marigolds — placing them along the back of the bed between the widely spaced green peony shrubs for contrast. Clumps of mixed colors in large and medium

71

zinnias were put in next, and for border plants we used blue and white petunias and a scattering of dwarf yellow marigolds. I filled one corner of the bed with several varieties of herbs. We began to see results by the end of June, and a few weeks later we were in full bloom.

Ordinarily, I eschew both marigolds and zinnias in favor of less stiff and more sweetly scented annuals. In this case the petunias helped offset that problem. This selection of flowers is most satisfactory for an expendable garden since little daily attention is necessary. The seedlings seems to grow in soil not especially good organically, and they do well near the ocean and the salty breezes. The strong prevailing winds are hard on the more delicate annuals, though blue salvia is rugged and grows quite rapidly, too. This is an example of how to have a simple and bright midsummer garden to look at without much pampering, especially with a rented house.

A Wealth of Bloom
in a Small Summer Garden
Ruth H. Metcalf

THIS picking garden covers about a ten by ten uneven square by the side of our house on the York River. Through part of July, August and September this tiny plot offers a colorful spot in the garden and a variety of flowers for the house; petunias, snapdragons, calendulas, asters and alyssum — and some years zinnias, statice and button dahlias, for all of these are good in bouquets and flower arrangements.

The garden is bounded on one side by a stone path; on another by a small pool; the third side, cedar trees; and the fourth, a stone retaining wall with a three foot drop to the lawn below. As you can imagine, the drainage is excellent. It is on the east side of the house and benefits from the full sun until three in the afternoon.

What weeds grow there when I arrive in June! After pulling them and raking, I am ready to fertilize. Ten pounds of bone meal, a half package of super phosphate, a five pound bag of 4-12-4 spread on the bed and forked in — this does the trick. Now it is ready for the annuals, and I plant them quite close together, even crowding them a bit. As soon as they are in the ground, I cut them back so that only a few leaves are showing.

It is hard to cut off the first buds — especially the first snapdragons and petunias, but this is going to make the plants bush out and produce more flowers. It also promotes the growth of a good root system. Then I water each plant thoroughly by hand with a mixture of water and Rapid-gro or other liquid fertilizer in the watering can — be sure to follow the directions on the label. This type of feeding is important for the young transplants will not sulk as much from shock. Then on goes the sprinkler for an all night watering.

Now for the bane of my summertime existence — woodchucks! Their favorite dish is zinnias. I've known them to devour every leaf on the newly set-out plants and leave only a pitiful skinny stem. A woodchuck is like a naughty child caught in the forbidden candy jar, for the second they see or hear you they run off to hide. Unlike children these little rascals hate water so never fear for your garden when the sprinkler is running or when it is raining. My all out warfare against these garden pests is a thorough dusting of each plant with arsenate of lead powder applied in the early morning after the all night soaking. I have a "squeeze box" type duster which is just an oblong cardboard box with metal ends. One end has a round opening and there are holes punched in the cover that fits it. It is simple, easy and quick to use — one squeeze sends out enough powder to cover a plant. I am sure I haven't killed any woodchucks — we still see plenty around — big ones, little ones and medium size too. They must know better — after one sniff of the dusted plants they go off looking for less highly seasoned greens!

At this point all I hope for is a week or more of sunshine — good growing weather. The garden requires very little attention. It must be weeded of course and I do this every few days with a hoe. If there is a heavy rain, the plants will have to be dusted again. At the end of ten or twelve days I sprinkle the plants with liquid fertilizer again, let them have another all night soaking and finish with the dusting in the morning. This can be repeated three weeks later but it may not be necessary.

Towards the end of July, the plants will be big enough to crowd out the weeds. The woodchucks will have learned their lesson and the garden will be full of colorful bloom. All that is needed now is picking and cutting off the dead blossoms. Don't let them go to seed for this cuts down the bloom. Just keep on picking.

Try a garden like this. It has worked so well for me that I am sure you will be pleased. Too, you may not have to cope with woodchucks!

❧❧

For the best in raspberries try "Amber," the color of its name, and "Canby," a large red berry. The canes of these varieties are nearly thornless, with enormous berries, and small seeds. The delicious, sweet, melting fruit is too soft for commercial purposes, so they must be grown in the home garden. They are truly ambrosial eaten warm and dead-ripe from the bushes.

❧❧

In colonial Salem, Massachusetts, "asparagras" was often planted as a hedge between front lawn or garden and the street. In this way, small city grounds could produce a delicious vegetable, and then enjoy a thick hedge which would keep out summer dust, offer privacy and beauty, and feed the birds with berries in autumn.

List of Hardy Perennials

Marion P. Hosmer

Blooming in May-June	*Height*
Alyssum saxatile (Basket of Gold) — Rock Garden, too	6 inches
Alyssum citrinum (Basket of Lemon) — Rock Garden, too	6 inches
Alyssum compactum (Dwarfer) — Rock Garden, too	4 inches
Aquilegia (Columbine) — All varieties — some Rock Garden	6 inches-3 feet
Arabis — Rock Garden	6 inches
Aubretia — Rock Garden	6 inches
Cerastium (Snow in Summer) Rock Garden	6 inches
Convallaria (Lily-of-the-Valley) — Good ground cover	6-10 inches
Euphorbia polychroma	18 inches
Hemerocallis (Day Lily) — Varieties may be selected to give a succession of bloom into October	1-3 feet
Iberis sempervirens (Perennial Candytuft) — Evergreen — Rock Garden, too	8 inches
Iris — Many varieties and species will give succession of bloom through August. Several Rock Garden kinds	4 inches-3 feet
Linum (Flax) — All perennial varieties — through July	1 foot
Mertensia (Virginia Bluebell) — disappears after blooming	2 feet
Paeonia (Peony) — All varieties — into July	2-3 feet
Papaver orientale (Oriental Poppy) — All varieties — through July	2-3 feet
Phlox divaricata — Rock Garden, too	1 foot
Polemonium (Jacob's Ladder) — All varieties	1 foot
Primula (Primrose) — Many varieties — many for Rock Garden	6 inches-1 foot
Pulmonaria (Lungwort) — Rock Garden, too	6 inches
Pulsatilla, syn. Anemone Pulsatilla (Pasque Flower) — Rock Garden, too	6 inches
Trillium — All varieties	6 inches-1 foot
Trollius (Globe Flower) — All varieties	1-3 feet

Blooming in June-July	
Anchusa azurea Dropmore	4 feet
Anchusa azurea Loddon Royalist	3 feet
Anchusa myosotidiflora	1 foot
Baptisia	2 feet
Centurea macrocephala	2 feet
Centurea montana (Perennial Bachelor's Button)	2 feet
Chrysanthemum leucanthemum (Shasta Daisy)	2 feet
Coreopsis lanceolata	2 feet
Delphinium Belladonna — all varieties	2-3 feet
Delphinium Grandiflorum — all varieties	1-1½ feet
Delphinium hybridum — all varieties	4-6 feet
Dianthus plumarius (Pinks) — and many other Dianthus varieties	6 inches-1 foot
Dicentra eximia (Plumy Bleeding Heart)	1½ feet
Dicentra Spectabilis (Bleeding Heart)	2-3 feet
Digitalis ambigua (Perennial Foxglove)	1½-2 feet
Gypsophila paniculata (Baby's Breath) — through September	3 feet
Hesperis (Sweet Rocket)	3 feet
Heuchera (Coral Bells)	1-1½ feet
Lupinum polyphyllus (Perennial Lupin) — named varieties	2-3 feet
Nepeta (Catmint)	1 foot
Penstemon caeruleus	1-1½ feet

Penstemon heteraphyllus True Blue — especially good 1-1½ feet
Phlox decussata — all varieties — through September 3-3½ feet
Pyrethrum (Painted Daisy) — all varieties 1-2 feet
Thalictrum (Various Rues) — all varieties — through September 3-5 feet
Thymus serpyllum (Creeping Thyme) — Rock Garden 4 inches-4 feet
Veronica — all varieties 1 inch

Blooming in July-August

Height

Achillea — all varieties	2-5 feet
Althea (Hollyhock)	6 feet
Astilbe — named varieties	1-1½ feet
Belamcanda (Blackberry lily)	3 feet
Campanula persicifolia (Peach-leaved bell-flower)	2½ feet
Catananche (Cupid's Dart)	2 feet
Dictamnus (Gas Plant)	2½ feet
Digitalis mertonensis (Perennial Foxglove-pink)	3 feet
Echinops (Globe Thistle)	3-4 feet
Eryngium (Sea Holly) — most varieties	1½-5 feet
Heliopsis (Sunflower) — some varieties	2-3 feet
Hosta (Plantain Lily) — all varieties	1-2 feet
Monarda didyma (Beebalm) — several varieties	3 feet
Platycodon (Balloon Flower) — all varieties	6 inches-2½ feet
Spirea — all varieties	2-6 feet
Stokesia (Stoke's Aster)	1½ feet
Thermopsis (False Lupin)	3-4 feet
Yucca filamentosa (Spanish Bayonet)	3-4 feet

Blooming in August-September

Aconitum Napellus (Monkshood)	3-5 feet
Artemisia lactiflora	3-5 feet
Asclepias tuberosa (Butterfly Weed)	1½-2 feet
Aster novae-angliae / Aster novae-belgii } (Michaelmas daisies) — all varieties	6 inches-4 feet
Boltonia	4-6 feet
Chrysanthemum koreanum — some other varieties — through October	10 inches-3 feet
Cimicifuga (Snake-root)	3-4 feet
Dierama (Wand Flower)	4 feet
Echinacea (Rudbekia-Purple Cone Flower)	3 feet
Eupatorium	2 feet
Galega Officinalis (Goat's Rue)	3 feet
Gaura (Butterfly Flower)	3 feet
Helenium (Sneeze-weed) — all varieties	1½-4 feet
Liatris (Kansas Gay-feather) — all varieties	2 feet
Lobelia cardinalis (Cardinal Flower)	3 feet
Lobelia syphlitica (Blue Lobelia)	2 feet
Physostegia Summer Snow (Obedient Plant)	2 feet
Physostegia Vivid (Obedient Plant)	2 feet
Sedum spectabile Brilliant (Showy Stonecrop)	1 foot

Blooming in September-October

Many plants indicated in the above lists	
Aconitum Fischeri (Fall Monkshood)	3 feet
Anemone japonica (Japanese Anemone)	2-3 feet

75

Mulching in Maine

Marion P. Hosmer

ACTUALLY this title is simply for the sake of euphony. The subject matter applies to the whole area. So much has been written in recent years about mulch, that these paragraphs will simply deal with a few experiences of my own that have proved helpful.

Being a New Englander, I usually have an eye to the thrifty way, and so feel that to make use of materials at hand is much cheaper and easier. However this is not the only reason that I use pine needles for both a summer, and in some cases, a winter mulch. Pine needles are easily gathered from woods and roadsides in early autumn, they are weed-free, clean, free from disease, attractive and do not blow. They can be used over, and added to, and they smell delicious. I use them as a permanent mulch on the peony and lily beds, and after the new strawberry bed is planted it is mulched with the fragrant needles. Before snow flies additional basketsful are heaped over the crowns of the plants, where they remain until May. Then the mulch is pulled aside a little, but still left lightly over the buds and blossoms to protect them against a late May or early June frost. Berries that ripen resting on the clean pine needles do not need the washing that takes away part of the flavor.

Sawdust and salt hay are two excellent mulches available locally for little or nothing. They also do not blow, and will last for more than one season. As they gradually rot down, humus is added to the soil as well as some nutrient, and a yearly application of fertilizer with a nitrogen count of 10 will keep the soil in good health.

I have tried both cocoa shells and buckwheat hulls and both are good-looking, and keep the soil in good condition. But both are expensive, the cocoa shells mildew and are unsightly then, and the buckwheat hulls blow away. Neither lasts for more than a year.

For trees and shrubs growing in a lawn, pebbles or crushed stone are effective. Remove the sod for a one-foot circle around the tree and fill the space with the stones. This conserves moisture, discourages mice from gnawing the bark and is a great protection from injury from the lawn-mower.

In this area with its short growing season it is very difficult to get melons to ripen, but black polyethylene laid down around the plants will warm the soil earlier, keep it warm, and protect the fruit from the rot that comes from contact with the soil. The black plastic is also excellent for tomato plants, and it is said that it will make them more resistant to early fall frosts.

Peat moss, the most advertised mulch, has a tendency to dry out and then becomes impervious to water, and also will blow. If you use it, get sphagnum peat and not the black Michigan peat, and dampen it before you try to put it on. Get a bale in the fall and let it stand out all winter, when it will be a good consistency.

The road crews here often cut and chip roadside brush, leaving it in piles, or taking it to a dump. This is an excellent mulch for all sorts of trees and for the vegetable garden; it can easily be removed from the latter and piled to use again.

Finally, I would enthusiastically recommended that anyone interested in mulch write to the Brooklyn Botanic Garden, 1000 Washington Avenue, Brooklyn 25, New York, for a copy of their "Handbook on Mulches". It costs one dollar and will save you many times that in time, labor and plant loss.

Garden Blights

Barbara Cheney

GARDENING, I told myself, is the most sociable of hobbies. The very nature of one's field of activities demands an audience. No one wants flowers to blush unseen or waste their sweetness. This was what I thought until last week.

Last week I worked hard, weeding, setting out new plants, dividing old ones. When at last I arose from my muddy knees, I felt elated, though weary, and eager to display the fruits of my labors. My first hope was an old friend who dropped in for tea. I restrained my impatience until she had been properly fed. Then I led her forth.

"Oh yes," she cried, "I'd love to see your garden. I'm so fond of flowers."

As we neared the scene of my triumphs, and I was slowing down to begin my introductory speech, she tucked her arm in mine and said, " I'm so glad to have a chance to chat with you alone. We have so many, many weeks to catch up."

"Yes indeed," I said vaguely. "Now here is the entrance, you see. I'm very proud of my iris. I planned these clumps myself so that I have three months of continuous bloom."

"How nice," she said. "Have you heard from Ann lately?"

"No," I said, thinking to block that detour. It was the wrong answer.

"Well, I have," said my guest, firmly planting her foot on my favorite sedum. "She's been to a psychoanalyst and has a new ego — not a very nice one, if you ask me." Nothing would have induced me to ask her, but that made no difference. I learned all about Ann's ego.

"We'll stay here by these clumps of iris until she looks at them," I thought, but I finally took pity on the sedum and led her on. Ann's ego absorbed her until we had passed the peonies, about which I was bursting to talk. At last she paused for breath.

"You must notice my Scotch broom," I said hastily. "It's very rare in this country."

"Did you know the Scotts were getting a divorce?" she asked. This time I knew better than to say no.

"Yes," I said, concealing my surprise, "I heard all about it." But that didn't work, either.

"Oh, did you?" she said. "I doubt if you know the whole truth. Few people do." The whole truth carried us past my violas, my prize lupins, my rare old pinks. The only interruption was when she fell over the watering pot.

"I didn't see it," she explained.

"No," I said coldly, "you weren't looking."

It was several days before I recovered from this interview. I chose my next visitor more carefully. She was a real gardener, deeply interested in gardens, and she approached mine as eagerly as I did.

"The hedge," I explained, "has not recovered from the terrible winter of 1962. It died right down to the ground."

"Don't talk to me about the winter of '62," she cried. "Do you know that I lost two box bushes that were a hundred years old, and that lovely Dr. Van Fleet rose that I planted myself in 1940?"

I expressed genuine sympathy and then began again. "I'm very proud of my iris," I said.

"Have you any Ambassadeurs?" she asked. "You must get some. Mine are beautiful. They actually stand almost three feet high. I have another new variety, too — Moonlight. It's perfectly beautiful."

I hurried her on to the peonies. "These I divided and set out myself," I said proudly, knowing that a real gardener would appreciate what a feat this was.

"You have no single ones, have you?" she asked. "I have the prettiest ones, pale pink, the Japanese variety. You must come over and look at them before they go by."

I was speechless after this, but she was not. My lovely blue lupins reminded her of her lovelier pink ones, my violas of the apricot ones she had at last achieved.

"Haven't you any dahlias?" she asked.

"No," I said firmly, "I hate them."

"Oh, but my dear, you wouldn't hate mine if you once saw them. The flowers are five inches across, they really are, and such lovely colors. I have some extra roots. I'll send them over."

"What I really want," I said to myself plaintively, "is someone who will look at my garden and think about my garden for just a few minutes. It doesn't seem too much to ask." It wasn't. I found her. She was the worst of all.

"I'm very proud of my iris," I began.

"My dear," she cried, "how beautiful they are! I never saw a prettier combination of colors. Those pale lavender ones next to the deep purple are perfect, and that touch of yellow adds just the right contrast." My soul began to expand.

"They are so perfect," she went on, "I think they ought to be where they would show off more. Couldn't you put them over there with the stone wall for a background?"

"The peonies are there now," I protested. "I set those all out myself. You have no idea what a job it was digging up the old roots and dividing them."

"Well, if I were you," she said, "I'd put the peonies over here."

"Yes," I said doubtfully, "but these lupins took five years to grow, and they don't move well once they're established."

"Oh, my dear," she said, "that's what the books tell you, but don't you believe it. You can move anything if you do it carefully. Speaking of moving," she went on, " I'm not sure I wouldn't move that hedge. It seems to me it would be more effective if you set it back about three feet."

"Next year," I said, "I'm going to have a new hedge, a very tall one, made entirely of thorns."

Safety Tips on Using Pesticides
(For Plants and People)

Cynthia Westcott
Croton-on-Hudson, N. Y.

1. Read the entire *label before opening* the container, noting all warnings and cautions. Do not inhale the vapor of the concentrated chemical; if any is spilled on the skin wash off *immediately.*

2. Always store in *original* container with label intact. It is not safe to share a pesticide with your neighbor.

3. *Keep all pesticides out of reach of children and pets.* A woman called to ask me how much chlordane to use on her lawn for grubs. She had left her creeping child and the open container alone together in the kitchen.

4. Never store pesticides in cabinets with food packages.

5. Destroy empty containers immediately. Bury cartons or burn them, keeping away from smoke. Wash out glass and metal containers before putting in the trash can.

6. When operating, keep out of the spray drift. Never smoke while spraying. After spraying, wash hands and face before smoking or eating.

7. Cover bird baths, dog dishes, fish pools before spraying. Never leave a pail of prepared pesticide open to children, pets, or birds. Put baits for slugs under jar covers or boards.

8. Pour leftover spray into a gravel drive, down a drain, or over soil. Never leave puddles on an impervious surface to attract birds and dogs.

9. Do not plant mint, strawberries, tomatoes and other edibles near ornamentals that may be sprayed frequently with pesticides.

10. Protect your plants. Use correct dosage and a fine mist to get as complete coverage with as little material as possible. Never spray to the point of run-off; don't drench the ground. Avoid oil sprays when the temperature is below 45°F. or above 85°. For plant disease, spray *before*, not after, rains and don't rush out to spray again as soon as the rains stop. Modern pesticides are formulated to stick until the next application is due.

Reprinted courtesy Manufacturing Chemists Association, Inc.

Useful Magazines

HORTICULTURE. Monthly. Illustrated in both half-tones and color. From the Massachusetts Horticultural Society, Boston. To non-members, $4.00 per year.

PLANTS AND GARDENS. Quarterly, excellent handbooks in color and half-tones. From the Brooklyn Botanic Garden, Brooklyn, N. Y. 11225. To non-members, $3.00 per year. Splendid back issues available at $1.00 each on Flowering Trees, Pruning, Mulching, Soil, Flower Arrangement and countless other subjects of concern to gardeners.

PARK'S FLORAL MAGAZINE. Monthly. In color and half-tones. A revival of a very informative horticultural magazine first printed in 1895. From George B. Park, Park's Floral Magazine, Greenwood, South Carolina 29647. $3.00 per year.

AMERICAN ROSE MAGAZINE. Monthly. Price included in dues, $5.50 per year to American Rose Society, 4048 Roselea Place, Columbus, Ohio. Their Annual sold separately to non-members.

ORGANIC GARDENING. Monthly. In half-tones. With emphasis on organic gardening and farming, but with invaluable information on soil, mulching, conservation, and with a garden almanac for each section of the country. From Rodale Press, 33 East Minor St., Emmaus, Penna. $5.00 per year.

FARMERS' ALMANAC. Yearly. Published for 147 Consecutive Years. Weather predictions, Tide tables, Planting by the Moon, Recipes and Sage Advice. From Farmer's Almanac, Lewiston, Maine. Price $1.00.

Standard Reference Books

Hortus Second, L. H. Bailey and Ethel Zoe Bailey, The Macmillan Co., New York, 1960.

New Illustrated Encyclopedia of Gardening (unabridged), Edited by T. H. Everett, Greystone Press, New York.

America's Garden Book, James and Louise Bush-Brown, Charles Scribner's Sons, New York, 1958.

The Gardener's Bug Book, Cynthia Westcott, Doubleday and Co., 1964.

Herb Gardening in Five Seasons, Adelma Grenier Simmons, Van Nostrand, Princeton, 1964.

Flower Arranging

Mechanics

Harriet Robeson

HAVE a "tool chest" with the proper equipment needed for flower arranging. The "mechanics" — the means by which you hold your arrangement firmly in place where and how you want it to be — is essential to know, even in home arrangements. Nothing is more discouraging than to find your effort failing to remain stable or falling out of line. In flower shows this immediately gives you a black mark. Also if any part of your mechanics show, the holder, any wires, etc., this again counts against you. Thus, the mastering of mechanics is "a must."

You will need a wide variety of flower holders, to suit your every container. Pin holders, of many sizes, seem to be the favorite; but there is also the cup shape with pins inside which holds water and is valuable for shallow containers; the cage type is very useful.

The first step is to anchor the holder firmly in the bottom of the selected vase by parafine or plasticine. Many arrangers keep holders permanently fastened down in the vases they use often — always ready for use. Experiment and you will soon find your favorite holders.

There are other ways of anchoring your flowers. Strips of soft plumber's lead are invaluable for fastening heavy stems and branches at the top of the vase. Soft hen wire (not chicken) crunched up in the top of the container will often save the day.

Keep in your tool box Twistams of varied lengths.

A spool of pliable wire.

Short pieces of florist's wire of varied weight and length.

Small pointed sticks with wire attached of varied lengths and strength. These are for strengthening and lengthening stems when needed.

A roll of brown and green florist tape to mend a break or cover a joining.

Here it is well to stress again, in competition, no holder, wires or obvious props can be seen. No matter how often judges disagree, they agree on this one point — a demerit for any sign of a mechanic.

Clippers of course — heavy for collecting your branches and flowers and definitely a light slender pair for "thinning out" your material when the arrangement is overcrowded. Overcrowding is a very common fault — avoid it.

Oasis is another means of holding flowers. Cut it to size and soak well for two hours or more until it absorbs enough water to keep flowers fresh. This also should be anchored in your vase.

Containers

Harriet Robeson

IF you have your own garden you are apt to grow flowers that look well in your home. Also you will find that certain flowers look well in certain vases.

Time and material will be saved if you have some idea of what you plan to do, where your arrangement will be placed and what your color scheme is to be. The less you handle your flowers the fresher and crisper will be your arrangement.

Never underestimate the importance of your container! Dedicated "arrangers" are always looking for new containers. Antiquing is a popular pastime. One can often find some odd or lovely vase, a sugarbowl, a tureen, even if shabby, that could well turn out to be your favorite vase because it fits into some spot in your home and holds flowers beautifully.

One can never have too many containers; make a hobby of collecting them. Especially if you have a garden full of flowers.

Glass containers range all the way from delicate cut crystal to the pickle jar saved for its lovely color green or for its interesting shape; never of course designed to be a favorite flower vase.

Marble and alabaster urns are generally more classic in shape and with their soft textures give great distinction to an arrangement. And pottery — so great a variety in shape and color and texture. Next to the flowers themselves come the container in importance in an arrangement.

We should not overlook the Gifts of the Sea; driftwood, shells, etc. A visit to the kitchen may unearth wooden boxes, chopping bowls, jugs, bottles and iron pots.

So never give up looking for containers!

BASES

Bases on which you place your completed arrangement add greatly to its finished appearance. There are almost as many kinds of bases as containers; some sophisticated, some very simple of wood or marble, some light and some dark in color. Often a piece of embroidery or brocade will tie the whole arrangement together. Sometimes the use of a base perfects the proportion of vase to flowers. Yet this is where many arrangers go wrong! Study this carefully for color and proportion.

Conditioning Foliage

Frances Earle

E FFECTIVE foliage is a very important part of flower arrangements and
should be considered accordingly. Select foliage with form, color and
texture in mind. Once selected and conditioned the foliage can be kept in
a semi-permanent arrangement, to which a few fresh flowers may be
added for emphasis, and quickly if necessary.

The foliage should be washed and submerged in cold water for an hour
or two. The older the foliage the longer the submersion. It should then
be carefully dried, put into a plastic bag and kept in a cool place until
time for use. Evergreens should be washed in soapy water and soaked
overnight.

Beech should have stems slit and put into hot water overnight.

Calla Lily foliage should be pin-pricked along the stems and put into
a tub of cold water.

Cyclamen leaves should be put into cold water overnight.

Ferns should be placed between tissue paper and wet thoroughly.
Curled, unopened fronds can be wrapped in water-soaked paper and
tied with string.

Some foliage may be preserved indefinitely by the use of glycerine,
though this will change the color and sometimes the texture of the leaves.
Foliage should be cut, the bottom bark scraped off, stems split and put
into hot water and glycerine — two parts water and one part glycerine to
about five inches — and leave for two to three weeks. Fall foliage is
treated in the same manner. The treatment is most effective if done in
hot weather. The glycerine solution can be kept for re-use, and as it is
expensive, narrow containers, such as Mason or mayonnaise jars with
wide mouth, are suggested.

Branches can be bent into desired shapes by handling them gently and
tying with string before conditioning. If stems are heavy leave out of
water until limp, then bend and condition. Evergreens and Scotch Broom
bend more readily if soaked in warm water.

Branches of nearly all trees are easily forced and are nice to have on
hand for arrangements. After a hard frost in January, select a mild day,
if possible after a rain, and cut the branches around noon-time. Choose
a long branch with large buds. Split the stem ends, scrape off the bark and
soak in a bathtub until conditioned. Then place in a pail of water in a
light room, out of sunlight. Add charcoal to the water or change water
regularly to keep fresh. If they should come too soon they can be retarded

by placing in a darker room in very cold water. As a general rule cut your branches six to eight weeks prior to the time you wish to use them.

(This treatment holds true for forcing branches of Forsythia, Dogwood, Japanese Quince, Apple, Flowering Crab and other fruit branches.)

Vines used for foliage are best conditioned if kept under water overnight. They can be tied into desired lines.

The foliage from many house plants are useful and effective in arrangements. Condition them in cold water as above.

Too often the new "arranger" fails to note the contribution of foliage in an arrangement. The use of it frequently means the difference between just another bouquet and an arrangement of distinction. Foliage can be used to establish a basic line or accent and can also serve to break the line of mass and heavy groupings of colorful flowers.

Foliage may form an entire arrangement in itself. There are myriad shades of green. Also great variety in textures. The combination of these can be as exciting as is brilliant color. There are straight lines, slender lines, curved lines, tendrils, heavy colored veining and stems as in chard and rhubarb; also velvety, soft or spiney angles. Leaves may be fully open or tightly rolled as in Cannas.

Experiment and watch for unusual foliage. Always consider line and remember you can train your foliage into lines as you would have them go. And remember also that garden flowers are often enhanced by foliage other than their own.

Conditioning Cut Flowers

JUST as foliage needs conditioning to prolong its life, so do cut flowers. Once a flower is cut from its parent plant its natural source of water is gone. You must replace that supply of water as quickly as possible and encourage the flower to take up as much extra water as the stem will absorb. Hence the importance of proper cutting and conditioning of your flowers before arranging them and thereby prolonging the freshness of your arrangement.

In preparing roses it is well to strip off all leaves below the water line and also strip the thorns; otherwise thorns may ruin your perfect leaves.

H. R.

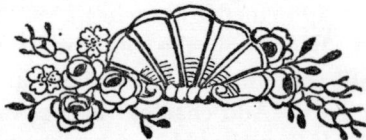

10 Ways to Add Hours to Your Flowers

By permission of the *New York State College of Agriculture at Cornell University*

1. Cut the flower stems. A freshly cut stem absorbs water freely. Use a sharp knife or sharp shears and cut either on a slant or straight across. Remove at least one-half inch of stem to expose a fresh surface.

2. Follow special procedures for special cases. A milky fluid flows from stems of some flowers when they are cut. This fluid plugs the water conducting tubes of the stem. To avoid this problem place about one-half inch of stem in boiling water for 30 seconds, or char the end of the stem in a flame. Protect the tops by wrapping them in paper.

3. Remove excess foliage that will be below water. Excess foliage increases water loss and submerged foliage decays and hastens cut-flower fading.

4. Use warm water. Place the stems in water at 110° F. Warm water moves into the stem easier and faster than cold water. Use a clean container for this hardening process.

5. Use a commercial flower food in the water. Flower foods are composites of sugars, acidifiers and mild fungicide, all of which increase the lasting life of cut flowers. The use of aspirin, copper pennies, or other similar remedies does not prolong the life of cut flowers.

6. Wrap the flowers until they are crisp. After you place the flowers in warm water, wrap a piece of paper or plastic around them. This cover prevents rapid air movement over the flowers and reduces water loss from them. After the flowers become crisp (about two hours) you may arrange them and they will continue to take up water. If the flowers wilt, repeat treatments 1 through 6.

7. Wash the container with soap and water. Containers should be washed after each use to remove bacteria. Bacteria multiply and clog the water-conducting tubes of the flower stems, causing premature wilt.

8. Avoid excessive heat. Do not place flowers in direct sunlight, over a radiator, on a TV set, or in a draft. Heat reduces flower life. Warm or moving air takes water from flowers faster than it is absorbed through the stems.

9. Keep flowers cold when not in use. Double the life of your flowers by placing them in a cold room or refrigerator at night, or when not in use. Any temperature from normal room temperature to 35° F. will pro-

long flower life. Orchids and Gladioli, however, should not be subjected to temperatures below 50° F.

10. Do not mix flowers with fruits or vegetables. Many fresh fruits and vegetables produce enough ethylene gas to shorten flower life. For example, Carnations close and Snapdragons drop florets prematurely when mixed with fruit.

My Annual Picking Garden

Ruth M. Putnam

IF you like flowers and like to have arrangements throughout the house, there is nothing from which you can get more pleasure than a picking garden, with a profusion of flowers in the colors and varieties that are your favorites and also practical for the locality in which you live.

For the State of Maine the season for annual flowers is about three months; it is not practical to plant plants until the end of May, and seeds perhaps a week or so earlier. There are several annuals that are pretty resistant to light frosts in the fall, so the following are good flowers to plant in this climate to extend the picking season as long as possible. They are: marigolds which come in a wonderful variety of sizes, colors and shapes; bachelor's buttons, cosmos, calendula, mignonette, blue salvia, nicotiana, pansies and petunias. It is always a surprise to see the zinnias turn black at the first light frost; they are so sturdy looking. However they are a must for the picking garden; nasturtiums are also a must but these will be lost at this same time.

In selecting your seeds be sure to get them from a reputable dealer and don't buy packages of mixed seeds, as the result can be quite chaotic. For my own garden I am particular in my selection and as I grow most of the flowers for the house I concentrate on those with which I can make harmonious arrangements and ones that will blend with the colorings in the house.

I use some seeds and some plants of annuals in flats which I buy from a first class nursery. I find a flat of a dozen plants planted about eight or ten inches apart make a good amount for one variety. This summer with one dozen snapdragons, I had all I needed and plenty to spare. Scabiosa was another variety that I bought in flats and was most satisfactory. There are about seventy-five annuals so it is possible to grow your favorites

It all depends on the size of your picking garden as to how many kinds of annuals you want to tackle. When they are well spaced, cultivated, fed and weeded they really thrive under these circumstances and there is no crowding as there would be if planted with perennials. Of course annuals among perennials are a must for color and a succession of blooms, but this article is for the picking garden and its merits.

I find a border of parsley and some lettuces make an attractive edging and a useful addition to the salad bowl. The parsley and lettuce can be bought in flats and for a later crop of lettuce one may sow the seeds along with the flowers the end of May. When sowing seeds they should be planted quite thickly as only about sixty percent germinate, so it is an easy matter to thin out if they come up thicker than you wish. It is important to thin the seedlings in a picking garden, leaving space for the plants to flourish, which they can not do when crowded. When you do thin it is always possible to move some of these plants into the border of the regular garden beds.

If you have a picking garden in connection with your vegetables it is easy to have good soil as a load of well rotted manure and a generous amount of bone meal put on in the fall and plowed or harrowed in the spring make a desirable bed to work with; otherwise a good spading and fertilizing can be achieved with foot work and elbow grease!

In the spring when I am planting my seeds and plants I add some dry manure and peat moss to the rows. Space the rows far enough apart so you can enjoy the space between for cultivating and picking.

There are so many lovely annuals and the catalogues so fascinating that it is a problem what to select; however don't go too far overboard and use the tried and true seeds with maybe an experiment now and then. True knowledge will come with experience and failures.

Good luck and good gardening.

Wild Flower Conservation Lists

WILD native material in our territory is a rich source for use in flower arrangements. Careful check should be made with State lists of material that may NOT be picked. Use of these would disqualify one's arrangement in any contest.

*WILD FLOWERS IN SPECIAL NEED OF CONSERVATION
No Wild Orchids Should Be Picked Or Uprooted

SPRING AND EARLY SUMMER FLOWERS
All Alpine Plants
Barren Strawberry — Waldsteinia fragarioides — clearings, woods
Bloodroot, Red Puccoon — Sanguinaria canadensis — rich woods
Calypso — Calypso bulbosa — bogs, cool woods
Canada-Violet — Viola canadensis — deciduous woods
Downy Yellow Violet — Viola pubescens — deciduous woods
Dutchman's-breeches — Dicentra Cucullaria — rich woods
Early Saxifrage — Saxifraga virginiensis — dry or wet rocks

Flowering Dogwood — Cornus florida — Acidic woods
Fringed Polygala — Polygala paucifolia — woods
Jack-in-the-Pulpit — Arisaema triphyllum — wet woods
Lady's-slipper — Cypripedium, ALL spp. — damp and dry woods
Liverleaf — Hepatica Americana — dry woods
Partridge-berry — Mitchella repens — dry or moist woods
Pinxter-flower — Rhododendron nudiflorum — woods, swamps
Pitcher-plant — Sarracenia purpurea — Sphagnous bogs
Pogonia — Pogonia ophioglossoides — Sphagnous bogs
Rhodora — Rhododendron canadense — cool bogs
Robin-run-away — Dalibarda repens — woods
Showy Orchis — Orchis spectabilis — mostly calcareous woods
Swamp-pink — Arethusa bulbosa — Sphagnous bogs
Sweet-Bay — Magnolia virginiana — swamps, low woods
Trailing Arbutus, Mayflower — Epigaea repens — sandy woods
Trillium — Trillium, ALL spp. — rich woods
Twinflower — Linnaea borealis var. americana — cool woods
Wild Columbine — Aquilegia canadensis — rocky woods or open slopes
Wood-Sorrel — Oxalis montana — mossy woods

SUMMER AND FALL FLOWERS

Canada Lily — Lilium canadense — wet meadows
Cardinal-flower — Lobelia Cardinalis — swamps, damp meadows
Clammy Azalea — Rhododendron viscosum — swamps
Coral-root — Corallorhiza spp. — dry and damp woods
Fringed Gentian — Gentiana crinita — meadows, brooksides
Fringed Orchis — Habenaria, ALL spp. — bogs, meadows
Grass-pink — Calopogon pulchellus — bogs
Indian-pipe — Monotropa uniflora — woodland humus
Ladies'-tresses — Spiranthes, ALL spp. — dry or moist open soil
Mountain-fringe — Adlumia Fungosa — wet woods, rocky slopes
One-flowered Pyrola — Moneses uniflora — cool, mossy woods
Pipsissewa — Chimaphila umbellata var. cisatlantica — dry woods
Purple Gerardia — Gerardia maritima — damp soil
Rattlesnake-plantain — Goodyera pubescens — dry woods
Sabatia — Sabatia, ALL spp. — brackish marshes
Spotted Wintergreen — Chimaphila maculata — dry woods
Sundew — Drosera spp. — wet peaty soil
Swamp Rose-Mallow — Hibiscus moscheutos — marshes
Turk's-cap-Lily — Lilium superbum — wet meadows
Wood-Lily — Lilium philadelphicum — dry, open clearings
Yellow False Foxgloves — Gerardia spp. — dry open woods

WILD FLOWERS
Which May Be Picked Freely

SPRING AND EARLY SUMMER FLOWERS

Blueberries — dry and wet places
Bluets — open, moist meadows
Bugleweed — roadsides
Buttercups — fields
Celandine — waste places
Coltsfoot — wet places
Cranesbill — Woodlands
Dandelion — fields
Gill-over-the-ground — roadsides
Golden Ragwort — wet meadows
Heal-all — roadsides
Hedge-Bindweed — dry soil
Mustard — fields
Robin's-plantain — meadows, open woods
Shadbush — low ground
Sheep-Laurel — swamps, old pastures
Stonecrop — dry open places
Violet — dry and wet places
Wild Lily-of-the-valley — woods
Wood-betony — woods, clearings
Yellow Lady's-Sorrel — roadsides
Yellow Rocket — wet meadows

Agrimony — woods, thickets
Asters — roadsides
Bedstraws — dry and wet places
Black-eyed Susan — fields
Blue Vervain — damp thickets
Boneset, Thoroughwort — moist places
Bouncing-Bet — waste places
Bush-Clover — sandy soil
Bush-Honeysuckle — dry clearings
Butter-and-eggs — dry fields
Campion — roadsides
Cat-tails — swamps
Chicory — waste places
Cinquefoil — dry fields
Clover — fields
Common Elder — damp, rich soil
Coneflower — rich, low ground
Daisy —fields
Daisy-Fleabane — waste places
Elecampany — rich fields
Evening-Primrose — dry soil
Everlastings — dry fields
Fireweed — recent clearings
Forget-me-not — wet soil
Golden Aster — sandy places
Goldenrods — open places
Hawkweeds — fields
Ironweed — wet meadows
Jewelweed — damp soil
Joe-Pye weed — damp meadows
Knotweed — roadsides

Meadow-Rue — wet meadows
Meadow-sweet — wet soil
Milkweed — waste places
Mints — moist soil
Mullein — dry fields
Partridge-Pea — dry soil
Pickerelweed — ponds
Pokeweed — recent clearings
Queen Anne's lace — waysides
Silverrod — roadsides
Sneezeweed — damp meadows
Spiked or Purple Loosestrife — marshy land
Spikenard — rich woods
Spreading Dogbane — dry thickets
Spurge — waste places
St. John's-wort — dry pastures
Steeple-bush — low ground
Stitchwort — wet meadows
Sunflower — waste places
Tansy — waste places
Thistles — waste places
Trefoils — dry woods
Vetch — fields
Viper's Bugloss — roadsides
Wild Cherry — roadsides
Wild Lettuce — rich woods
Wild Parsnip — roadsides
Wild Roses — dry and moist meadows
Yarrow — waysides
Yellow Dock — everywhere
Yellow Loosestrife — moist places

*Lists prepared by New England Wild Flower Preservation Society, Inc.

Mid-Summer Wild Flowers

Lois W. Forbes

MY mid-summer picking garden in Maine is the lovely area between two rivers, the Piscataqua and the Kennebec. Here I have found flowers, shrubs, and trees, closely related to those I discovered as a child when my world was limited to fifteen square miles in Minnesota. When I came to Maine with its ocean beaches and salt marshes, and its mountains (I now refer to Agamenticus) my scope of the genera in each wild flower family and its species, an individual plant within a genera, was widened.

I will restrict myself here to flowers that flaunt their elegance in July and August.

To insure prolonged happiness of the material, cut on the bias. From my mid-summer picking garden, I must have water for immediate immersion. I fill and place in my car one to five rectangular red plastic pails, one for branches, one for short-stemmed material, another for longer ones, one for material miserable to touch, wild roses, thistles, burdock, barberry — each one first cornucopiaed into newspaper. Sometimes into this pail I will heavily wrap a perfect bloom for a definite vase. Lastly, always one pail for the melee of things unexpectedly seen, each bunch of just one species, bound within a rubber band. These are often flowers unimportant if used singly or with stems too weak for a holder.

One quickly learns picking material that gives one continued satisfaction. Leaves that curl within 24 hours or so do not enhance the beauty of flower or fruit, I remove before I cut. If a choice, I pick those with flower heads just breaking into bloom. I have decided what containers are to be used and pick accordingly. With fingers and wrists festooned with colored elastic bands and strong red-handled cutting shears looped on one finger, I sally forth to course the roadside. Flowers on the conservation list, I admire; others I gather with abandon. A new flower pushes me into ecstasy. Sometimes I wonder why I've never spotted it before; the blue toad-flax (*Linaria canadensis*) I found this year growing in dry sandy soil so unimportant with its small blue two-lipped and spurred flower, ⅓ of an inch long. Do not use singly; cut plant at its base and bind with an elastic band and use as an accent of blue.

Butter-and-eggs (*L. vulgaris*) with its one inch flower, if crowded into a low old polished diamond shaped brass receptacle, picked up years ago in Utrecht, and placed on the dining table, always say "Thank you." Wild flowers do not seem at home in clear crystal — one exception, a very thick smokey glass, modern in shape. They respond to simple classic shapes, pottery, tins set in plaited palm leaves from Hawaii, ancient Chinese bronzes, woven baskets, pewter, bamboo or any container without a design.

My favorite time for my wanderings is early in the morning, before the sparkling diamonds of dew have been dissipated by the sun; birds sing, and the whole world seems refreshed and rejoices.

Sometimes I drive directly to a spot which harbors certain plants — maybe something has caught my eye that I wish to examine in a more leisurely fashion; sometimes my aim will be water-loving plants or plants that thrive in damp moist meadows, or on river banks, or along streams and salt or fresh water marshes. Sometimes I play a game, collecting from rich, thin or rocky woodlands, in fields, sandy and dry, borders of woods and shaded roads just one color.

I had no idea that there were so many midsummer pink flowers. The spiked meadow sweet (*Spirea latifolia*), each flower like a miniature apple blossom, hardhack or steeple bush (*S. tomentosa*), thimbleberry, the flowering raspberry (*Rubus odoratus*), the wild pasture rose (*Rosa carolina*); the *R. rugosa*, so happy along the sea coast; bouncing bet (*Saponaria officinalis*); white campion (*Lychnis alba*) with its five styles and pink inflated calyx; the low growing campion or wild pink (*Silene carolina*) with its three styles; the many clovers: *Trifolium pratense* most common with its fat globular flower-head and its leaflets, marked by a whitish triangle — Vermont's state flower (*T. hybridum*); rosy pink and shorter stemmed Alsatian clover, most fragrant of all (*T. arvense*); the deliciously fuzzy one, rabbit foot or stone clover — this I also pick in bunches securely tied and later combine with self-heal (*Prunella vulgaris*). One must search for the pink yarrow (*Achillea millefolium*) and pink Queen Anne's Lace (*Daucus carota*). The common vetch (*Vicia sativa*) with its lacy leaflets soften my bouquet. The beach pea (*Lathyrus maritimus*) I never combine with other plants. Wild thyme (*Thymus serpyllum*) will be relegated to a shallow bowl and sparked with shortened stems of burdock (*Arctium minus*) — all leaves snipped off — and the water loving many jointed knotweed which I also have found growing lushly around fresh water bound pools on the Isles of Shoals (*Polygonum hydropiperoides*). Lady's Thumb with its smaller rosy pink spikes (*Polygonum Persicaria*), so very common in shaded waste places, I never bother to use. Herb Robert (*Geranium robertianum*) with its 3 to 5 distinct leaflets, tinged in red, and with their ruddy stems, and long-beaked seed vessels, I push into the stretched elastic.

In low wet ground or in ditches or in marshes there are hosts of joe-pye weed with dense terminal flower clusters (*Eupatorium purpureum*); the purple spiked loosestrife, each flower with four petals (*Lythrum salicaria*) with opposite leaves not to be confused with fireweed, the great willow herb (*Epilobium angustifolium*) with alternate leaves and a ruddy stem that quickly takes over recently burned ground, and the swamp loosestrife (*Decodon verticillatus*), a shrubby plant not as effective with its flower clusters growing from the lance-shaped nearly stalkless opposite leaves. Pink turtle head (*Chelone Lyonii*) and the pink tinged *Chelone glabra* are not as easily found. The false dragonhead (*Physostegia virginiana*), a perennial, prefers open fields.

Light grey green linear leaves follow up the stem and terminate into a chartreuse dome, which if examined are the bracts that center a very insignificant flower of the spurge (*Euphorbia Cyparissias*). When severed, it annoints my hand with its sticky milky juice and I must wash immediately. When using this spurge I like to set it off with deadly nightshade stripped of all leaves, its small potato-shaped flower clusters with a 5-lobed corolla, a rich purple, centered by the 5-stamens, a sharp yellow, that forms a cone (*Solanum Dulcamara*). This can be sparked also with the cups of pure yellow of the cinquefoil (*Potentilla recta*). Too sad never to pick chicory (*Cichorium Intybus*)! At midday in full sunshine have you ever had the good fortune to observe its strong energetic second blooming, after a scythe has cut it to the quick when it carpets the floor in violet blue and is interspersed with the short flat heads of Queen Anne's Lace (*Daucus carota*)? One might add the early goldenrod (*Solidago juncea*) with yellow-gold heads spread like an elm, or *S. canadensis*, the most common one, with its greenish golden yellow plume-like clusters or the very earliest, its flower cluster also plume-like but reclining, its leaves sharp edged, *S. Arguta*.

Maybe this is the time to discuss a very few of the 60 species of the goldenrod. I immediately think of the seaside goldenrod (*S. sempervirens*) with its long showy heads and stout smooth stem, the dwarf alpine found on Mt. Agamenticus (*S. Cutleri*); the most brilliant one (*S. nemoralis*) with its one-sided plume rising happily to 2-4 feet in dry pastures and along sandy roads; *S. odora*, the anise-scented one, also one-sided. I have been aware of, but seldom pick *S. rugosa*, rough stemmed, light in color, and widely branched like an elm, or *S. gramminifolia*, lance leaved with flat topped flower clusters. I prefer the late one, *S. gigantea* with its plume-like lilac bloom bending at its top or *S. speciosa*, with its dense somewhat pyramidal showy flower clusters. I am not tempted to seek the bog goldenrod (*S. uliginosa.*)

Background materials easy and quick to use are our state tree, the white pine (*Pinus strobus*), five needles, 3-6 inches long; or high or low bush blueberries, huckleberries, bayberry (*Myrica caroliniensis*), and the common juniper (*Juniper communis*), with its prickly needles, and *J. Virginia* with its blush blued berries. The thick velvety white green of the basal rosetted leaves, if properly seasoned, of the great mullein (*Verbascum Thapsus*) add texture and strength to an arrangement. Often I will dig it up, roots and all, before it sends up its flower-spike, and use for the focal point (with its roots in water it will persevere for some time). Each year I push the golden buttoned tansy (*Tanacetum vulgare*) into a large brass container jammed with white pine.

Tasseled grasses of various lengths too weak to stand alone must be bunched and tied.

Plumes of shimmering red top; timothy grass or the common cat's tail (*Phleum pratense*); wild oats (*Avena fatua*); false oats (*Arrhenatherum elatius*), its spikelets brown to green to lilac on a metallic lustre when flooded with full sunshine; the common quaking grass (*Briza media*) is a joy for a joy for a child to gather and blow upon, as its loose panicles with straggling branches with egg-shaped delicately balanced spikelets of a purplish brown hang from long hairlike branches, so slender as to cause continuous tremulous motion; the sea matweed (*Psamma arenaria*), clumps of which can be transplanted to hold down drifting sand; meadow barley (*Hurdem pratense*), with its compact upright much-awned spikes, two inches long, prefers dry sandy areas. One must move on to wet moist meadows and marshes for the marsh bent grass (*Agrostis palustris*) with its graceful, cone-shaped panicles pale yellow to purple; the elegant spreading millet (*Milium effusum*); the airy delicate slender silk bent grass (*Avena spica-venti*); the quivering drooping hairy brome-grass (*Bromus racemosus*). Too many bur reeds — the great, the smaller, the branchy, always erect, their fruit a burlike sphere, looks like a miniature pineapple, leaves ribbonlike; and too many rushes to list, the bulrush (*Scirpus lacustris*), a favorite with its tufted top; the black bog-rush (*Scirpus nigricans*), with tufted spikelets crowded together into a head, held in by a pair of opposite bracts; and too many sedges, but I do favor *Carex arenaria* that grows in sand, at the sea or at fresh water lakes, the beach clot bur, now so unprickly; its fat elongated, unripened burs bunched at the end of its stem are soft to touch and in color are a fine yellowish green.

Avidly, I have stretched out over a pond to break off branches of the button bush (*Cephalanthus occidentalis*), a shrub 5 to 20 feet tall with its fuzzy creamy ball-shaped flowers — when placed in city water, its ball quickly collapsed. The ground nut or hog peanut is much more obliging (*Apios americana*); it is a vine that clambers over roadside shrubs stretching out for the sunlight. It is unbelievably fragrant, its velvety, bean-shaped, drooping round flower clusters are maroon to pale brown lilac.

Yellow pond lily or spatter-dock (*Nuphar advena*) and white water lily (*Nymphaea odorata*) are always out of reach.

Climbing vines, I have used running down the length of my dining table, virgin's bower or old man's beard (*Clematis virginiana*) or climbing wild cucumber (*Echinocystis lobata*) both produce delightfully shaped seed vessels. Bitter-sweet (*Celastrus scandens*) with twisted stems and loose fruit clusters, a green green, can be used in a line arrangement.

I have never found anything that combines pleasantly with the erect cattail (*Typha Angustifolia*), the narrow leafed one grows in our marshes close to the coast; the broad leafed one (*Typha latifolia*), common everywhere, has even greeted me in South Africa.

Foliage plants that I use time and again are the rues, the earlier one (*Thalictrum dasycarpum*), its stem often stained magenta; the most common one with its misty soft adorable starry clusters of white flowers (*Thalictrum polygamum*); the deeply cut grey leafed *Artemisia absinthium*; sword shaped leaves of the blue iris, the blue flag (*Iris versicolor*); the heart shaped wild ginger leaves of *Asarum canadense*, or anything at hand that will serve the purpose of the day.

Sometimes I deviate and can be drawn into the woods, there I find the fruit pods of the early spring flowers, the Jack-in-the-pulpit (*Arisaema triphyllum*) its spadix clustered with bright red fruit; the red baneberry (*Actae rubra*) with its red oval berries; the white ones (*A. Alba*), its white fruit with its purple black eye; the false solomon seal (*Smilacina racemosa*) 1-3 feet high, its pea shaped fruit, a soft tan, speckled with madder brown; the wild false lily-of-the-valley (*Maianthemum canadense*), 3-6 inches high, its berries very much like the above-mentioned plant; the *Clintonia borealis* with its round "true blue" blue fruit, or the ghostly white nodding Indian pipe (*Monotrapa uniflora*) that shows disapproval when picked by turning black; or the delicate wood sorrel with pinky veined 5 notched petals which Fra Angelico and Sandro Botticelli have painted so charmingly. The shinleaf (*Pyrola elliptica*), waxy, greeny white flower with a long pistil bending downward; or on a rotted stump the creeping twinflower (*Linnea borealis*), the most delicate pink bell-shaped flower of the woods. Too intent am I to escape a stinging nettle (*Urtica dioica*) or shy away from beggar-ticks (*Bidens frondosa*) with its two-pronged seed vessel not yet firm enough to attach itself to me. A covey of bunchberry (*Cornus canadensis*), its white flowers (which really are bracts) or with scarlet tightly packed fruit whorled with curving ribbed leaves, always means Maine to me.

There is a wealth of material on Agamenticus: the various heaths — checkerberry (*Gaultheria procumbens*) evergreen aromatic leaves and small vase shaped waxy white flower; Bearberry trails hither and yon (*Arctostaphylos Uva-Ursi*) with its pinkish bell-shaped flower; the creeping snowberry (*Gaultheria hispidula*) with its wintergreen-flavored tiny stiff leaves and its nodding white flower; the small wintergreen (*Pyrola minor* or *P. secunda*) (not a heath) 3-9 inches high with flower stalk, and its one-sided greenish white flowers; the one-flowered wintergreen (*Moneses uniflora*) very much like the shinleaf only smaller, 2-5 inches high; and the partridgeberry or twinberry (*Mitchella repens*) that snuggles closely to the earth; Lapland rosebay (*Rhododendron Lapponicum*). In season, cranberries and blueberries grow here and en route choke-cherries (*Prunus virginiana*) can be picked and later combined with apple if jelly is to be made.

Along the marginal way in York Harbor the scarlet pimpernel (*Anagallis arvensis*) can be found. It is a temperamental flower opening in full sunshine, closing in rain, and in England it is called "the poor man's Weatherglass."

In hurricane woodlands, the wild sarsaparilla (*Aralia hispida*) flourishes, an angular plant with handsome umbel-tipped delicate light chartreuse flower — later its round fruit is a deeper chartreuse and by the end of the summer becomes a huckleberry black. Here the red wood lily (*Lilium philadelphicum*) asserts itself. I know a meadow where yellow lilies spotted purple-brown grow (*Lilium canadense*) and another place for the more orangey buff-colored Turk's cap lilies (*Lilium superbum*) which lift their regal heads above the grass.

Have you ever picked the tall yellow clover (*Melilotus officinalis*) or the white one, (*M. Alba*) to dry and then place on your closet floor to permeate the allotted space with its fragrance?

The good old dependable favorites for bouquets are the white oxeye daisy (*Chrysanthemum leucanthemum*), black eyed Susan (*Rudbeckia hirta*), blue spiked vervain (*Verbena hastata*) with its four-sided stem; the lavender blue marsh speedwell (*Veronica Scutellata*); the pearly ever-lasting (*Anaphalis margritacea*) wooly with papery white petals; yellow hawkweed (*Hieracium scabrum*); the orange one (*H. auranteacum*); wild lettuce (*Lactuca canadensis*); the shrubby St. John's-wort with opposite leaves (*Hypericum perforatum*) and a golden starred flower with many stamens, the shorter one with ochre yellow flowers (*H. denticulatum*), not to be confused with the yellow loosestrife (*Lysimachia quadrifolia*) its four leaves encircling the stem bearing a single star on a fine stalk; the *L. Terrestris*, so like the above, carry their flowers in spiral-like clusters; the yellow ten-rayed sunflower (*Helianthus decapetalus*); the deep golden ragwort (*Senecio aureus*); the showy dock (*Rumex venosus*) in all stages can be picked (always remove all leaves); the shorter one *R. Acetosella*, 6-12 inches, turns a ruddy brown.

My new find of 1963 was the smooth white *Pentstemon laevigatus var. digitalis*, 2-3 feet high in open woodlands, and picked only that once, as I've never come upon it growing in great profusion.

I have been aware of, but not attracted to, the seaside heliotrope (*Heliotropium curassavicum*) with its one-sided coiled spikes of white. I can miss the misty sea lavender or marsh rosemary, a salt marsh plant, that dried beautifully (*Limonium carolinianum*) because its very assertive ground cover is the low growing *Salicornia* which presents a rich glow to the low salt flats.

In late summer there is boneset with its dull white florets in terminal clusters (*Eupatorium perfoliatum*), I had thought might be white snake-root (*Eupatorium rugosum*) its flowers very white and similar to our garden ageratum. If I find a yellow yarrow, I pick it, to dry, as it keeps its true color. The tall ironweed with a rough stem (*Vernonia noveboracensis*) carries flower heads of bristled tips of madder purple, each one like a rayless bachelor's button. The tall flat-topped white aster umbellatus or any of the 65 species is closely related to the goldenrod (never with yellow flowers); Hemlock parsley (*Conioselinum chinense*); the wild parsnip (*Pastinaca sativa*) and the cow parsnip (*Heracleum lanatum*) with its very large flat clusters enjoy moist or wet ground.

I have rattled the seed box of *Crotalaria sagittalis* on the Isles of Shoals. Fortunately, there are not as many milkweeds here as there are in

South Africa. One might wonder, when passing me, what I would be doing. The milkweeds stand, stripped of all leaves, and at each break there is a white ball of its thick, sticky milk. After this is done, I give each stalk a shake, then I cut and hurry them to a pail of water. The common one (*Asclepias syriaca*) has a wide variation in color from brown, lilac, pink to yellows. Later if I pick to dry their fascinating seed pods, I place hair nets over the pods so that when they burst, their seeds can not be wafted out into the room. The fake milkweed (*A. Exalta*) an ivory white, is a beauty and more so, when in full bloom, as their sepal-like corollas turn back. The one with the most intense color is *A. purpurescens*, often a pure crimson.

And so you have a list, all named flowers have been placed in vases in my cottage — throughout the long pleasant mid-summer days. Keep on the watch, and soon you too will have as much fun as I have had throughout the years.

Bibliography:

A Pocket Guide to Wild-Flowers, Samuel Gottscho, Washington Square Press, Inc., New York, 1960.
Wild Flowers to Know and Grow, Jean Hersey, Van Nostrand, Princeton, 1964.

Dried Arrangements for "Winter Bouquets"

CONDENSED by the Editors from three articles by our own members on "Drying Flowers" — Margaret Gerrity, Virginia R. Glendinning and Elizabeth R. Bockstoce.

Dried arrangements are synonymous in our thinking with the winter months when most of us depend on florists for fresh flowers. It is well to remember, however, that these dried decorations are "made" in the spring and summer months. Begin to collect your material as soon as the spring buds swell. Pussywillows must be picked before the pollen shows yellow, and Cattails should be picked when small and firm. Some material may be gathered both early and in the autumn for varied coloring, such as Chinese Lanterns and Dock. Of course, all the pods develop late, such as Acorns, Burrs, Clematis (large flowered) Cones, Locust, Day Lilies, Trumpetvine, Iris and Poppies. Look also for stems of Euonymous, Grape, Woodbine, and Wisteria which will often provide the "lines" so important in arrangements.

Nearly all the summer flowers may be processed for "Winter Bouquets" and much garden and wild foliage and grasses as well.

To harvest and process these materials four rules should be followed:

1. Harvest on a sunny day. Never after rain or heavy dew. (Exception is Cockscomb.)

2. Harvest more than you expect to use because loss is high.

3. Start the preserving process as soon after the gathering as possible. Keep in deep water until processing begins.

4. Harvest at the peak of bloom (never later) save for Thistles and Everlasting which should be picked *before* fully out.

There are four tested and successful ways of drying your material.

a. Hang upside down to dry in a dark place. If attached to a wire coat hanger stems are separated making them stronger than when dried in a bunch.

b. Many-petaled flowers are more complicated to dry. The most successful mixtures to work with seem to be a combination of borax with cornmeal or sand — three parts sand to one part borax — or six parts white cornmeal to one part borax. Experiment yourself for best results. Have your mixture one inch deep in bottom of a large flat box. Remove all foliage from stems. Cut stems five inches long and run a florist's wire up the stem bending a small hook on end. Wire can be pulled back into heart of flowers and does not show. This should be done before drying when stem is soft and flexible.

Place flowers face down on top of mixture, carefully pouring from spoon in and around the petals. Rosettes of Mullein for example come through better if leaves are separated by small pieces of crumpled paper while drying. Flowers will dry from one to three weeks. To quote from an experienced "dryer" — "You will find flowers brilliant in color and the petals velvety in texture."

c. A more recent product, Silica Gel, is now popular for drying flowers, as they stay quite true in color in this medium. Use it in the same way as with borax and cornmeal, tin cans tightly closed are required for the drying process. Follow directions on the Silica can. The flowers may be faced down or up. Spike flowers such as Delphiniums and Snapdragons should stand spike upright in a tall can or jar; and the Silica poured gently between the individual flowers. Do not over dry. It is necessary to experiment; removing flowers too soon results in wilting shortly after removal. Leaving too long results in flowers becoming very brittle.

Clean off sand, borax and silica very gently by blowing or using a soft camel's hair brush. Wrap stem and wire with florist's tape and pack lightly in large boxes until used. Almost all colors hold fast. Some reds and pinks may turn purple and become less attractive. Experience will guide you.

Some rosette forms dry better on a picket holder or on crumpled newspaper so that outer leaves or petals drop a little and the whole gives the effect of a half or full-blown flower.

d. Anything that can be used flat, press between newspapers and put under a heavy rug or board to dry.

It is essential to keep all dried material in rooms free from dampness and bright sunlight. Dampness ruins substance and sunlight fades color.

And once more — process twice as much material as you think you will need, because it is very fragile.

To Dry Leaves

PICK when green and lay on newspaper in a hot dry place. When spread they should not touch each other. Once a week turn on other side. It is important to get all moisture out before packing away. When thoroughly dry lay on newspaper in large flat boxes and cover.

All other plant material stand upright in large containers without water. Large tin cans used for fruit juices can be used. Weight down with stones. Keep in a hot dry place. Any heavy texture leaf will dry. You will find there is much plant material that requires no attention other than being arranged in the desired position and left alone until dry. This is true of straight forms such as cattails, seed pods of iris, poppy, peony, veronica, grape hyacinth, dock, mullen stalks and grasses. Leaves of gladioli, iris, day lily preserve their straight lines by putting in narrrow containers that hold them straight until dry.

The curved and twisted forms such as bitter sweet, wisteria and all curling tendrils it is best to arrange and let dry in place.

Other material which can dry into three dimensional forms and give curves and angles to add interest to arrangements may be inserted upright in pricket or hairpin holders until dry.

Suggestions for Material to Dry

Virginia R. Glendinning

I. To Hang Up To Dry —

Straw Flowers	Meadow Sage
Calendula Officinalis	Veronica
Heather	Yarrow
Celosia	Golden Ragwort
Celosia Golden Fleece	Sea Holly
Jewel Box	Snow in Summer
Veronica Maritima	Shasta Daisy

Everlasting
  (pick before mature)
Sea Lavender
Meadow Sage
Honesty
Joe Pye Weed
Dock — Spring green —
  midsummer pink
  September rich brown —
  Dry upright in container
  without water.

Globe Thistle
Cockscomb
Statice
Dusty Miller
Lavender
Baby's Breath
Grasses
All seed pods

II. Cured by Borax or Silica Gel —

Zinnias
Pansies
Abutilon
Roses
Delphinium
Larkspur

Marigolds
Calendulas
Dianthus Plumarius
Dahlias
Hydrangeas
Chrysanthemums

Experiment — Almost all flowers can be cured.

III. To Dry Flat — Pressed between Newspapers —

Ferns of many kinds
Lupin leaves
Croton leaves
Canna leaves
Wild Geranium

Sorrel Bush
Decodon
Purple Cabbage, single large leaves.
Some of the treated leaves can rest flat also.

Books on Flower Arrangement

THERE are many excellent books on Flower Arrangements on the market so this subject per se will not be dealt with in detail in this volume. However, since this is of general interest to all Garden Club members, we have asked three well-known lecturers and judges to list books which in their experience they consider most valuable for reference, covering elementary mechanics to the most advanced arrangements.

Mrs. Elizabeth Rhoades Reynolds of Sharon, Connecticut, says her selection is not necessarily the best books on Flower Arrangement, but are the ones that have proved most useful to her in answering questions that come up in classes, or in answering specific problems in relation to Flower Show exhibits.

The Arrangement of Flowers — Mrs. Walter R. Hine.

**A History of Flower Arrangement* — Julia S. Berrall.

The Complete Book on Dried Arrangements — Ray Miller Underwood.

How to Make Cut Flowers Last — Victoria R. Kasperski.

Complete Book on Flower Arrangement (very useful for beginners) — Rockwell & Grayson.

Many shows call for arrangements 'in the manner of' or 'inspired by' the Japanese School.

Stepping Stones to Japanese Floral Art — Rachel E. Carr.

Flower Arrangement Art of Japan — Mary Cokely Wood.

And for color classes.

Color in Flower Arrangement — Adelaide Wilson.

Mrs. Lawrence N. Wilson, North Ferrisburg, Vermont, suggests books she believes are specifically adapted to our northern area because most of the materials used are familiar and easily grown here.

Flower Arrangement Work Books No. 1, No. 2, No. 3 (small but invaluable)* — Myra J. Brooks.

The Magic Book of Flower Arranging — Myra J. Brooks with Mary Alice and John Roche.

New Horizons in Flower Arrangement — by Myra J. Brooks with Mary Alice and John Roche.

Flowers and Table Settings — Julia S. Berrall.

Miniature Flower Arrangements — Lois Wilson. (First of its kind and a treasure!)

Mrs. Anson Howe Smith, Dedham, Massachusetts.

Design in Flower Arrangements — John Taylor Arms and Dorothy Noyes Arms.

Favorite Flowers — Constance Spry. (This is Constance Spry's last book and is, I think, her best. Hers is always a creative approach and her sense of material is extraordinary. A book to own and to read often.)

Period Flower Arrangement — Margaret Fairbanks Marcus.

An Eighteenth Century Garland — Louise B. Fisher.

Chinese Flower Arrangement — H. I. Li.

Modern Ikebana — Edited by Seika Nishizaka.

Flowers in Glass — Julia Berrall.

*Indicates titles suggested by one or both of the other lecturers.

Unusual Flowers to Plant
for Use in Flower Arranging

Marion P. Hosmer

Achillea Coronation Gold	Perennial	Yellow
Allium—several varieties of onion family	Perennial bulb	Various colors
Anemone coronaria—several var.	Bulb, treat as annual	Various gorgeous colors
Antirrhinum Tetraploid (Tetra Snapdragons)	Annual	All colors but blue
Aquilegia (Columbine) McKana Hybrids	Perennial	Mixed colors
Argemone (Prickly Poppy)	Annual	Mixed colors, good foliage
Baptisia	Perennial	Blue—good seed-pods
Belamcanda (Blackberry Lily)	Perennial	Orange—good seed-pods
Bergenia	Perennial	Bold foliage
Bocconia (Plume Poppy)	Perennial	Grey foliage—good seed-pods—spreads!
Calendula "Geisha Girl"	Annual	Easily grown from seed—like an orange chrysanthemum
Celosia cristata (Cockscomb)	Annual	Mixed colors—dries
Clarkia (named for Lewis & Clark)	Annual	Many colors
Clematis—all good	Perennial vines	All colors — flowers, foliage and seed-pod
Cobaea scandens	Annual vine	Two colors, blue & white —effective
Coleus (mixed)	Annual foliage plant	Beautiful colors
Cynoglossum Firmament	Annual	Heavenly blue
Dahlias — various dwarf varieties	Annual tuber	All colors but blue
Delphinium Belladonna	Perennial	Comes in blue & white
Dianthus—many varieties	Perennial & Annual	All colors but blue
Didiscus (Blue Lace Flower)	Annual	Like blue Queen Anne lace
Echinops (Globe Thistle)	Spreading Perennial	Steel blue foliage & globular flower
Eryngium (Sea Holly)	Perennial	Steel blue throughout
Gaillardia—various	Annual & Perennial	Yellows & Reds
Gladiolus (small flowered)	Annual bulb	All colors except true blue
Godetia	Annual	Satiny flowers in most colors
Gomphrena (Globe Amaranth)	Annual	Most colors—dries well
Helenium	Perennial	Autumn shades

Helianthus (Sunflower)	Annual	Dwarf, double and single—easy
Hosta—all varieties	Perennial bulbs	Beautiful foliage
Lilies—many varieties	Perennial	May now be planted in spring in pots
Lunaria (Honesty or Money Plant)	Biennial	Flowers & seed-pods
Martynia (Unicorn Plant)	Annual	Interesting fruit
Moluccella laevis (Bells of Ireland)	Annual	All green—dries
Nigella (Love-in-a-Mist)	Annual	Blue—white—rose
Papaver (Poppy) somniferum	Annual	Stunning flowers and foliage—plant where they are to grow—get seed from England
Penstemon—many varieties	Annual & Perennial	Many colors—spikes
Ranunculus—many varieties	Bulb, treat as annual	Many colors — double and single round blossoms
Ricinus (Castor Oil Plant)	Annual	Striking foliage
Rudbeckia (Cone Flower)—many var.	Annual & Perennial	Autumn shades
Salvia — many varieties	Annual & Perennial	Investigate the new kinds
Scabiosa—many varieties	Annual & Perennial	Many colors
Sedum—many varieties	Perennial	Interesting foliage and good flowers—various colors
Statice—many varieties	Annual & Perennial	Many forms and colors—dries
Stokesia	Perennial	Large blue aster
Tagetes (Marigold)	Annual	Many new kinds of this old flower in new shades and forms and odorless
Talinum (Coral Flower)	Annual	Slender and dainty
Thalictrum—several varieties	Perennial	Rue-like foliage which takes on lovely colors in fall—good airy flower-heads and seed-pods
Thermopsis	Perennial	Yellow spikes of pea-flowers
Tithonia (Mexican Sunflower)	Annual	Brilliant autumn shades

Many ornamental grasses both annual and perennial may be found in most catalogues.

Particularly recommended for catalogues are

Thompson & Morgan Ltd. Ipswich, England	Joseph Harris Co. Moreton Farm Rochester, N. Y.	Geo. W. Park Seed Co. Greenwood, South Carolina

Winter study of these catalogues will suggest many new plants to grow, and those may be chosen which give you the size and color that will best suit your needs. It is interesting and fun to grow different flowers of the same shades and use them in combination.

Vegetables and Herbs to Grow for Arranging

Marion P. Hosmer

Scarlet runner beans — for the blossom

English Broad Beans — for the blossom

Purple Pod Royalty Bean — for the beans

Red Cabbage

Savoy Cabbage — crinkled foliage

Early Purple Head Broccoli

Royal Purple Broccoli

Indian Ornamental Corn

Strawberry Corn

Basil, Ornamental Dark Opal

Borage

Dill — Flowers, foliage and seed pods

Sage

Lavender

Kale, Vates or Dwarf Blue Curled

Kale, Flowering

Onion Sets, for foliage and blossoms

Parsley, Paramount

Swiss Chard, Burgundy

Small Fruited Tomatoes
    Red Cherry
    Red Pear
    Yellow Pear
    Yellow Plum
    Ground Cherry

Rhubarb — for stems, flowers and foliage

Okra — for flowers, foliage and fruit

Chives for flowers — dries well

Eggplant, Morden Midget — for flowers, foliage and fruit

Various Mints — for foliage

Indoor Gardening

Spring Indoors

Ala Reid

NOTHING is more welcome, when everything is still covered with snow, than a pot of spring bulbs. For flowers throughout the winter you need spend only one afternoon potting bulbs. All sorts of spring favorites may be forced. Among the small bulbs, muscari (grape hyacinths), chionodoxa (Glory of the Snow) or snowdrops are all good. Crocus are easy, but they collapse too quickly for me. These small bulbs do best in shallow bulb pans rather than regular pots — try a mixture! Easily forced daffodils include February Gold, Mt. Hood, Carlton, Trivithian, Geranium and the graceful little Thalia. This collection includes all types of daffodils whatever your fancy. If you want to try your hand at tulips, stick to the easier, early April varieties, either single or double. When potting tulips, always place them so that their flat sides face out and your pots will look much more professional. Of all bulbs, the hyacinth is my favorite for forcing. I always think it's at its best in a pot, its delicious fragrance filling the room. The trick with hyacinths is not to buy the Jumbo size bulb advertized for forcing, but the next size smaller. You can put more of these in one pot, and the slightly smaller heads won't topple over as easily. White is the easiest color, pink and blue next, and yellow and orange the hardest, but even if they don't look perfect they always smell wonderfully!

In September or early October, gather together some pots, your choice of bulbs and a good potting soil. An ideal soil is one third each leafmold, sand and loam. For the best show the pot should be in proportion to the ultimate size of the flowers, and the bulbs should fill the pots completely — almost touching the sides of the pot and each other. Provide plenty of drainage and fill the pots so that you can set the bulbs with their tips just an inch below the rim. Fill in between the bulbs, just barely covering their noses, and firm the soil around with your thumbs. This way, the bulbs are at the proper depth and you have left yourself enough room to water. As you finish each pot set it in a pan of water until the top is damp.

The next step is to find a cool dark spot for the bulbs while they develop their roots. The ideal place is a cold frame. After the bulbs have been watered just put them in and cover them generously with leaves. Any mulching material will do, but nature provides all those leaves just when you need them!

If you have no cold frame there are several possibilities. You can dig a trench in the ground, put your pots in that and cover them. The trouble with trenches in York is that you may never be able to pry the pots out of the frozen ground — if you can find them at all! If you have wells around your basement windows you can put the pots in them, and perhaps have the added advantage of being able to get at them from inside. A very ingenious solution is to stand the pots on trays of damp peat moss inside the bulkhead leading to your cellar door. If you can supply none of the above, pick the coldest, darkest corner of your basement and start them there. If you use either of the last two methods the pots will need water from time to time.

After you have put the Christmas decorations away and the house looks very bare, it is time to check one or two pots for root development. The smaller bulbs will be ready sooner than the larger ones, but you should tap them out to have a look. Turn the pot over, your hand covering the contents, and rap the rim of the pot on a handy edge. Everything will drop into your waiting hand and you can lift off the pot. If your pots are well along, you will see a maze of roots all through the earth ball. They are then ready for the next stage — a cool light place. When you put the bulbs back in the pot, bang the bottom down hard to settle the contents back down where they belong. For a succession of bloom take only a few pots at a time, the rest will keep. A greenhouse is the perfect next spot, but I have a cellar window that is very good, and a sunporch is wonderful too. If you have none of these a north window will be adequate. It is best to keep the bulbs at this stage until they are about to bloom. If you move them to warmth and sun too soon they tend to get very leggy and no amount of staking will keep them neat and compact like the florist's. Don't forget to water!

As your bulbs are about to bloom give them full sun wherever you will enjoy them best. After they have finished blooming keep watering the foliage sparingly until you can add them to your garden to bloom again for years to come.

Fun With House Plants

Gertrude B. McCarthy

HOUSE plants can be a great joy if wisely chosen for the conditions in which they are to be grown. It takes a little trial and error to determine which varieties will thrive. Most flowering plants like all the sun they can get in the winter, especially begonias, coleus, geraniums, orchids, hibiscus and browallias.

Geraniums are easy to grow, do well on window sills in full sun for several hours a day, and should be pot-bound to produce large flowers. They will bloom winter and summer for several years if the flowers are picked before they get old and it helps a great deal to cut long branches which can be used in flower arrangements. In this way the plants are pruned, keeping them compact and making them bloom more profusely. The more pruning the better they will grow.

Once a month is often enough to fertilize most plants and the earth should be very wet before fertilizing to be sure that burning does not take place. On sunny days plants are so thirsty that they sometimes require watering twice a day, but on cloudy days it is better to give very little water. Over fertilizing may produce luxurious foliage with very little bloom and pots which are too large for the plants may do the same thing.

Many foliage plants will do well in a location without sun if the foliage is sprayed with water and the plants are soaked about once a week. For about five years I have had plants growing in pots, which are set into a planter over an island in the center of a kitchen, which has a north and an eastern exposure. Once a week the pots are put to soak and the leaves get sprayed. This treatment has kept them in very good condition. In the collection are kentias or palms which are very practical for a warm room. Aspidistras do well, too, because they have an iron constitution as do the sansevierias. Philodendrons grow profusely and have to be pinched back quite often to keep them from trailing too far and they will adapt themselves to the conditions of the average home. Pothos does exceptionally well in this location.

Plants grown and forced by the florists are sometimes hard to care for in the house but are well worth the trouble it takes. Azaleas will do well year after year if they are planted in the pots outdoors in the shade of evergreens during the summer months if they are given plenty of water during June and July. They should be taken into the house in late August before the heat is turned on so that there won't be too great a change in temperature. It is well to keep the buds picked off during the summer so that they will bloom freely in the house in a sunny window.

Gloxinias are easy to grow with a western exposure if kept damp but not too wet. They can rest, after the blooming period is over, in a darkish place by withholding the water gradually. After a few months, new leaves will appear, when the plant can be brought into the light and watered sparingly until the plant is well established and ready to bloom again. Gradually it should have more and more light. There are many other plants which can be rested and carried over.

Growing plants or vines add greatly to the charm of any room.

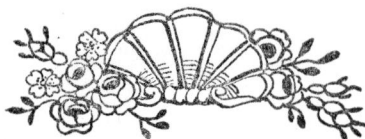

Sansevieria, I Love You

Muriel Howells

When friends deplore
The endless chore
Of keeping plants around the house
That soak up water like a souse
Just answer: "Here y'are!
Try Sansevieria!"

This long-lived plant
Is one that can't
Cause grief. It grows at a steady pace
With water and charcoal in the vase.
Others are temporarier
Than Sansevieria!

Its stems grow tall.
And this is all:
Provide some liquid food for it
On rare occasions when you see fit.
This plant will bury ya!
Hail, Sansevieria!

Mrs. Howells has kept the same graceful bouquet (of a narrow dark green variety) of Sansevieria in water for over five years!

House Plants — Hit or Miss

Margaret R. Cutter

SOME responsibilities are thrust upon us, some just grow like Topsy. I unexpectedly found myself in the position of having to manage a commercial apple orchard. I was anxious to succeed, as people were ready to tell me that I could not. I am not a horticulturalist. I have always had a mañana attitude and lethargy toward such things as spraying on schedule, fertilizing at the proper intervals, pruning and weeding. There is no mañana about growing fancy apples in competition, and so I was brought up with a jerk and had to grapple with nature on her terms. It was heaven coming to Kittery Point to live; a house by the sea, no land, no apples, no garden, no problems. This is the way I want it, I said to myself. My small piece of real estate consists of ledges, steep declivities, and little soil. It certainly was a mess when I took it over; a bit of tidying up was in order. Yes, you've guessed it. Every available inch is under cultivation, or soon will be. Having experienced the wonderful alchemy of the soil, how it soothes and strengthens in times of trouble, how it enhances beauty and happiness in times of gladness, I found that I couldn't do without actual contact with Mother Earth.

A new facet was recently added to my garden activities through the inspiration given me by the Piscataqua Garden Club. Their summer projects introduced to me the window sill garden. Hitherto almost all house plants have curled up and died under my ministrations. The first Club project in which I participated was the espaliered rosemary which continues to grow in the shape of a ball giving generously of its crisp fragrance. The ivy tree came next. In spite of my conviction that ivies in my hands immediately played host to mealy bugs and aphis, lost their leaves and died, my Club tree has burgeoned and even won an award. A valuable demonstration was made in connection with these two plants, which I have found helpful. That is the use of wire coathangers in making supports for plants in various shapes and sizes. The small success I had with these two ventures led to a reappraisal of the science of growing house plants. I state loudly and firmly that I won't give house room to any plant that doesn't like me, or disapproves of my treatment. However, I have found that most plants not only do well, but propagate so easily that I am being gradually pushed out of my house. For a birthday present I was given a plastic ring with a perforated cover. I use it on my dining room table, filled with clippings from my various house plants, and presided over by a colorful ceramic bird, as a focal point. In no time at all my bits and pieces had long trailing roots. Come spring I potted them. I was unable to throw them out. It is a problem to find space for them.

For the benefit of any of our readers who may want to grow house plants with the minimum of trouble, I will list my hit or miss methods for what they are worth:

1. If the plant or the plant variety doesn't like what you have to offer, throw it out.

2. Read all your house plant books. Among them you will find many contradictions. Follow the suggestions that are easiest for you.

3. Don't be afraid to put plants where they are not supposed to be. I have had success with north windows for plants claiming to need sun.

4. Chop off their heads! It is remarkable what beautiful full plants you achieve through ruthless pruning. Put the pruned pieces into water and you will find that most of them will sprout.

5. Water as to their needs. Train your forefinger to recognize dampness or drought.

6. Fertilize once a month. I choose the first Sunday of each month. I use a liquid fertilizer in the water, changing the formula once in a while. Most plants seem to thrive whether it is recommended or not.

7. Give foliage a bath once in a while and look for aphids, or any other unwanted troubles. I spray with Raid.

A few suggestions about potting may be in order. I always buy sterilized soil. I try to have dried oak leaves on hand to crumble in the bottom of the pot, a suggestion given us by Mrs. Taylor. The soil should be well soaked before using as it is dry as dust and difficult to wet down in the pot.

I have made many mistakes. I have, in my impatient way, been careless in my repotting methods. I have mutilated loved ones and mourned their passing. No such tragedies can mar my pleasure and enjoyment of their brothers and sisters which, by resisting my heavy handed ways, bring the out-of-doors inside to brighten the winter months.

The plants which tolerate my treatment are: Ivies, Wandering Jews, Geraniums and Ivy Geraniums, Succulents, Echiverea, an ungainly avocado raised from seed, the ubiquitous philodendrons, cacti and an herb or two.

‿ℳℴ

If you have a wide border that becomes trodden down because you have to step into it to work, lay a large stepping stone at strategic spots. The plants around these stones will grow better than the others because the soil stays moist under them, and broken plants and dirty shoes will be avoided.

Watch for the trees to leaf out if you want to forecast the summer's weather:
> Oak before ash,
> You'll just get a splash.
> Ash before oak,
> You're in for a soak!

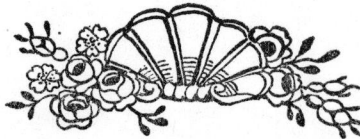

Natural History

Native Plants for Landscaping

Radcliffe B. Pike,
University of New Hampshire

NORTHERN New England gardeners have never made much use of native plants even though many have desirable ornamental qualities. Probably there are several reasons for this but possibly the chief one is because they are not easily available as nursery grown plants. Nurseries as a whole do not carry them because not enough customers ask for them. This leaves the ordinary gardener with the choice of collecting from the wild, which in many cases is undesirable; propagating them from seeds or cuttings or, as is usually the case, going without. Collecting from the wild can be a rescue operation if earth moving projects are about to destroy desirable plants. Saving of desirable native material under such circumstances can be considered conservation in the fullest sense.

The skilled gardener or interested nurseryman can raise many of our native shrubs from seeds or cuttings with ease, others with some difficulty. Plants so raised are superior to collected material in several respects but primarily because of the compact root system which develops due to the several transplantings involved in the cultivation procedure. If propagation is from cuttings this makes possible the selection of superior parent stock and the duplication of the superior qualities in the resulting plants. Seeds may or may not reproduce qualities found in the parent due to natural genetic variability. However, the choice of seeds or cuttings will usually depend on which method is easier or quicker for the particular species.

Strangely enough, shrubs or woody plants found in bogs or swamps often make the best garden subjects of any of our wild material. This is probably due to the need of these plants for full sunlight with no overhead shade rather than to supersaturated moisture requirements. Once established in ordinary garden soil these bog shrubs make better growth and are more attractive than under the rigorous conditions and stiff competition of their natural environment. One needn't have a so-called wild garden in order to use native shrubs, for they fit as well, if not better, into regular landscape planning than the introduced or exotic shrubs. Indiscriminate collecting from the wild must be frowned upon and discouraged except for rescue operations which will save plants that would otherwise be destroyed or crowded out.

The use of chopped sphagnum moss as a medium for germinating seeds or rooting cuttings greatly simplifies either of these operations and the additional practice of placing the containers (pots or flats) in plastic bags gives controlled moisture conditions with a minimum of attention. These techniques are worth learning because they enable the amateur to do on a small scale what only the professional could formerly do. Following is a list of native woody plants and shrubs useful in northern New England gardens, with pertinent notes.

Plants and Shrubs

Rhodora (*Rhododendron canadense*)

Found in bogs and heaths — flowers lavender to purple — very rarely white in early spring. Neat, dense growth — grey-green summer foliage — brilliant in fall. Up to 3 feet or even more. Full sun — acid soil — plenty of humus — peat moss. If transplanting take block of soil — cut back severely — propagate from suckers or stolons — seeds very fine — seedlings slow.

Leatherleaf (*Cassandra*) (*Chamaedaphne calyculata*)

Bogs and heaths — good but not spectacular — retains foliage which is bronze in winter — early white flowers on underside of twigs — two feet, eventually possibly four. Culture same as Rhodora.

Sheep Laurel (*Kalmia angustifolia*)

Bogs, heaths or dry soil — evergreen but turns brown if exposed to winter sun — flowers bright pink in June. 18 inches to 4 feet — further north the better — culture and propagation and care same as Rhodora.

Bog Laurel (*Kalmia polifolia*)

Bogs — rarely over 1 foot high, often only inches — small clusters relatively large attractive pink flowers June, July — good narrow foliage — desirable dwarf shrub — the only Laurel that is practical to propagate from cuttings — culture same as Rhodora.

Bog Rosemary (*Andromeda glaucophylla*)

Heaths and margins of bogs — unusual evergreen foliage — delicate pink blossoms terminate twigs in spring. Mildly stoloniferous — usually not over a foot tall — uncommon and desirable — easy from cuttings — culture as for Rhodora.

Swamp Honeysuckle (*Rhododendron viscosum*)

Bogs and swamps — white tubular sweet scented clustered flowers streaked on outside with carmine — sticky to touch — July. Foliage attractive summer and fall — usually 5 or 6 feet rarely to 15 feet — easy from seeds — fair from greenwood cuttings in July — best from numerous small seedlings usually found under parent plants — culture as for Rhodora.

Mountain or Swamp or Election Day Pink or Pinxter (*Rhododendron nudiflorum var. roseum*)
Wet or dry pastures — swamps, lake shores or margins of woods — without much doubt our most beautiful native shrub and by some considered the world's most attractive deciduous azalea — various shades of clear pink — fragrant flowers in June — from 3 to 6 feet — easy from seed — with luck from greenwood cuttings in July — adaptable to most conditions — highly desirable, culture as for Rhodora.

Black Alder — Winterberry (*Ilex verticillata*)
Swamps — our most northern holly — excellent summer foliage that turns black with frost — twigs on female plants lined with scarlet to orange red berries — very rarely a yellow fruited plant occurs. 6 feet or more rarely to 10 feet or more — winter decorations — birds — nearly impossible from cuttings — uncertain from seeds — best from suckers or division — once established does well — seemingly indifferent to location or soil.

Ink Berry (*Ilex glabra*)
A very unholly-like holly with evergreen leaves (often blackish in winter) and black berries — very rare native — neat mounded growth from 2 to 6 feet — usually available from nurseries — protect from winter winds.

Hobble Bush (Incorrectly Dogwood) — *Viburnum alnifolium*
In mixed woods and margins of woods — shade — gracefully informal or sprawling shrub with large ribbed heart-shaped leaves — flowers white (very rarely pink) in early spring resembling hydrangea — bright red berries in fall turning dark — leaves turn yellow orange and purple. 2 to 4 feet, sometimes more — slow from seed — easy from rooted layers — greenwood cuttings — distinctive — beautiful — should be in light shade.

Rose Bay — Great Laurel (*Rhododendron maximum*)
Most exotic looking and spectacular of northern New England shrubs — found in sheltered, shaded isolated areas often on margins of swamps associated with hemlock, red maple and birch. Flowers in early to mid July — apple blossom pink to white with no purplish tones. From a few to 15 or more feet. Easily propagated by either seed or cuttings from current season's growth. Also available from nurseries as either nursery grown or collected material. Wind shelter, some shade, adequate moisture

and highly organic, acid soil are essential for optimum development of this aristocrat of New England native shrubs.

Canadian Yew (confusingly known as ground hemlock) (*Taxus canadensis*)
A little appreciated yet widespread evergreen shrub of desirable habit. With shorter needles and of less robust habit than the familiar Japanese Yew of nurseries it has a more graceful manner of growth. However, in sunny locations it becomes bronze in winter. Hard to transplant except in small sizes. It is best propagated from cuttings which any nurseryman familiar with evergreens can easily accomplish. May bear fleshy bright red fruits as any yew may. The fruits, while pleasant to some people, are repulsively slippery to most which is probably just as well because the large seed contains a poisonous kernel.

The common or Pasture Juniper (*Juniperus communis*)
Which has overgrown so many neglected New England pastures is a superb dwarf shrub for landscaping and garden use. The sharp needles of an interesting combination of silver, green and bronze form an armor that discourages marauders either two or four-footed. The berries of green, steel blue and navy blue are usually abundant on female plants and are highly decorative. Small plants are easily transplanted, large ones with great difficulty. Wear gloves. Indifferent to soil or exposure as long as full light, best in direct sun. Mature stature varies from a few inches to a few feet, exceptionally there are upright pyramidal forms to 10 or 15 feet. Very easily propagated from cuttings by anyone who understands evergreens. This enables the multiplication of a wild specimen that suits your particular need and taste.

Bayberry and its close relative Gale or Sweet Gale — (*Myrica pennsylvanica* and *Myrica gale*) are two neat growing shrubs with superior foliage characters completely hardy for northern gardens. The bayberry is taller growing with larger foliage that is almost evergreen in some locations. The pale, grey berries are modestly decorative and are favorite food for small birds, especially the Myrtle Warbler which takes its name from this plant and may remain during the fall until berries are gone. The Sweet Gale is a generally smaller rounded shrub that will spread into a broad colony rarely over 3 feet high. The foliage is a glaucous grey green with a perfume almost identical with that of the bayberry. Both shrubs are difficult to transplant because of the ramifying root systems unless heavily pruned. If purchased they should be acquired as potted material to ensure survival of transplanting. Both shrubs are better without trimming unless they overgrow their location and that's the gardener's fault for putting them there in the first place.

Mountain Holly (*Nemopanthus canadensis*) grows around lake shores and streams as well as in glades in coniferous woods. It is not a true holly although closely allied to that genus. The brilliant, almost neon-red berries on long stalks are decidedly decorative from midsummer on. The oval foliage is attractive and the growth habit is neat. Eventual height may be 10 feet. Very adaptable as to soil or exposure. If transplanting cut back severely and take a ball of soil.

The American Highbush Cranberry (*Viburnum trilobum, V. americanum, V. oxycoccus*) is not easily distinguished from the European interloper *Viburnum opulus*. If the plants are in fruit the berries from our American plant are pleasant, if acid, while the berries from the European bush are disgustingly unpleasant in taste. When the shrubs are in leaf the two can be told apart by the small glands on the petiole or leaf stalk. Those on the American highbush cranberry being dome or club shaped while those on the undesirable European plant are cup shaped. Incidentally, plant lice may almost destroy or at least deform the European plant and yet leave ours alone. Give plenty of space to this 10 to 15 foot (or even more) shrub to display its great beauty of flower foliage and fruit. It is truly an all season shrub. Completely amenable to soil and exposure but for greatest results fertilize generously. Propagate from hardwood or greenwood cuttings or more slowly from seed. If purchased insist on a guarantee of the right species.

Potentilla, Cinquefoil or Golden Hardhack (*Potentilla fruticosa*)
A modest shrub of not more than 3 feet with five-parted grey-green foliage flowering heavily in early summer and less abundantly throughout. The flowers are about the size and color of buttercups and contrast pleasantly with the leaves. Almost every character of this shrub commends it for garden and landscape use in New England. Propagation is by any sort of cutting even in the open garden. Some lime should be available. Transplanting easy when it can be found, usually in alkaline pastures. Nurserymen may offer plants less hardy than our native species.

GROUND COVERS

There are several native plants that make superb ground covers although they may present somewhat of a challenge to gardeners until established.

Mountain or Highland Cranberry (Swedish Lingonberry) (*Vaccinium Vitis-Idea var. minus*)
A miniature broad-leaved evergreen only a very few inches high. Pink tinged white bell-like blossoms in spring and brilliant red berries in late summer and fall. Spreads by underground stolons forming thick mat —

121

very high humus acid soil — peat moss and/or rotten sawdust promote rapid spread — ammonium sulphate for fertilizer. Transplant by sods — easy to propagate by root cuttings, also by seeds if somewhat tedious. Excellent near seacoast or high elevations in full sun. In other locations some shade beneficial.

Bearberry (*Arctostaphylos Uva-Ursi*)

Trailing shiny-leaved evergreen of great beauty adapted to open sunny situations and sandy gravelly soil. Very difficult to transplant. Should be purchased as pot grown plants. Slow to spread until root system is well established but then will occupy an area very completely. Worth the care and time necessary to bring to vigorous growth. Adapted to almost any part of northern New England.

Bunchberry (*Cornus canadensis*)

An herbaceous dogwood that may carpet the ground completely. From the typical dogwood flowers in spring to the brilliant scarlet berries of fall a plant of great beauty. It does its best in northern latitudes the further north the better. Spreads by underground stolons and may rapidly occupy available space when conditions are suitable. Thin shade from deciduous trees seems to produce maximum flowers and fruit. Needs acid soil — mulch desirable — fertilizer ammonium sulphate. Propagate from root stolons — more uncertainly from seed. If transplanting, take clumps or sods.

Crowberry (*Empetrum nigrum*)

A prostrate evergreen with needle-like foliage found on coastal headlands and bogs and on mountains in exposed open situations where there is little competition from higher vegetation. Makes a dense fine-textured mat with trailing stems. Will grow on pure peat and makes a delightful and unique ground cover where well grown. Well adapted to northern New England. Easy to propagate by cuttings of the runners. Acid soil.

Ferns

Mary Stark

FERNS create a lovely greenery in many delicate shades and endless forms, which have beautified the earth since time immemorial. Many existed in the early land vegetation of the Devonian period and now appear as fossils. Today there are many thousand species.

The history of ferns is interesting. They are in the second great division of plants, the Archegoniatae, intermediate between the aquatic Thallophytes and the terrestrial Spermatophytes, the third great division of seed plants, which includes the flowering plants and the conifers. Thus they occupy a middle position in the evolutionary progress of plant life in which the remarkable transition from life in the water and life on land took place. It was a great step in evolution, when seeds were established.

Among non-flowering plants, ferns and their allies represent the highest development. They are not reproduced by seeds, as are flowering plants, but by spores. The spores are borne in spore cases on the under side of the frond in various forms and positions. The tiny spores are clustered in fruit dots called sori. Each sorus is usually covered by a lid called an indusium, which falls off when the spores are ripe. A notable characteristic of ferns is that the leaf or frond is rolled up in the bud with the tip at the very center and this is unique.

Most ferns are quite easy to grow. They need plenty of moisture and protection from the direct rays of the sun, but they must have drainage, and all but a few garden ferns like a soil mixture of equal parts of leaf mold, garden loam, coarse sand and peat moss.

In general they need much the same care as other plants. The great majority have fine roots close to the top soil and should not be cultivated. Sand or leaf mulch will hold in the moisture. Through the cold months it is well to leave the dead fronds and stubby bases to form a natural protection. Spraying with bordeaux mixture will control most fungus troubles.

Ferns may be increased by root division. Those which form a compact crown may be cut apart. Many of the common ferns, and there are endless varieties, have creeping roots, which may be cut apart and transplanted. Some have creeping rhizomes, which may be cut apart and a section held down until firmly rooted.

When transplanting ferns in a rock garden, the hole should be deep enough — at least twelve inches, so that the roots will have sufficient room. Rock ferns require a less rich soil than border ferns. Native ferns should be transplanted in the spring. When the ground is wet the roots are not so liable to dry out.

We have ferns about the shady side of our house, a northeastern exposure, which have come up every spring for over twenty years and fill these difficult spots with their lovely overarching fronds, creating a feathery greenery all summer long. So we feel very grateful to these particular ferns, for they have given us pleasure and satisfaction with very little care.

The Fern Guide by Edgar T. Wherry, Ph.D., Doubleday and Co., 1961, is a valuable handbook on ferns, their identification, habitat, and culture.

Getting to Know the Birds

Ruth M. Putnam

I F this short article does nothing more I do hope it will arouse more
people to interest in birds, bird watching and feeding. It is all such
an important part of our gardens and places to encourage them to stay
with us, and do their jobs which are many. Though there is more and
more interest in bird watching, there is still room for expansion and it
is so important for the amateur to learn to identify the species. I have
heard more people with feeders acknowledge that they don't know half
the time what their birds are. This is such a pity as there is always a chance
of something rare arriving, and it is great fun to be the "first" on some
new bird in the neighborhood.

It is now possible to get bird supplies almost anywhere, from super-
markets to hardware stores — seeds and suet made up into cakes and
balls, feeders of all kinds so now no one can use the excuse that they
cannot find materials. Besides winter feeding, it is recommended that
one continue through the year. There will not be so much activity during
the summer months, but it does keep the birds around the garden. During
the summer it is not always too easy to see the species to identify them,
with all the heavy growth of shrubs and leaves, but what is seen is often
rewarding and there is always the possibility of more nesting birds. Of
course all birds are not seed feeders and there is all the more reason to
encourage those that are not, as they will enjoy the worms and insects
that destroy some of our plants and flowers; and to encourage them to
be there is a great boon to the gardener, and I might add, a great pleasure.

One's interest in birds can (besides just being a home birder) expand
into a large area for the energetic birder, professionals and bird banders.
The latter, who contribute very important information on bird habits,
migration, etc., have to have State permits which are issued by the Fish
and Wild Life Service of the U. S. Department of the Interior. It is fascinating reading to see some of the reports on banding — the place where
banded and the place where the birds were found later. If anyone in the
State of Maine should find a bird with a band the information should be
sent to the Portland Society of Natural History, 22 Elm Street, Portland,
Maine.

I should heartily recommend subscribing to the *"Maine Field Naturalist"*
at the above address. It is published monthly and has a great deal of
interesting and informative material for any lover of nature. Another
publication that I would recommend is the *Massachusetts Audubon*
published by the Mass. Audubon Society, South Great Rd., South Lin-

coln, Mass. The best book for the beginner, in fact for any birder, is "*A Field Guide To The Birds*" by Roger Tory Peterson. This book really is a must; it fits into a coat pocket and is not too bulky to take on a walk. The other very important accessory is a good pair of binoculars.

A second book "*The Natural History of the Birds of Eastern and Central North America*" by Edward Howe Forbush and John Richard May is a good book to have at home for more detailed references.

When you put up your feeders for the birds, unless they are actually attached to the house, it is advisable to put them in such a situation that the birds can use a tree or shrub to "make the landing". They like to perch around in trees near the feeders, very often waiting their turn to fly down for the meal. Besides man's kindness in feeding the birds there is no doubt that they get a great deal of nourishment from all the wild and also cultivated fruit-bearing shrubs and trees. Red cedar, juniper berries, bayberries, elderberries, and sumac are all good winter fare.

Just before a winter storm it is noticeable that the birds sense the approaching bad weather and stock up on food at this time — be sure there is plenty of seed and suet for them as there will be great activity at the feeders.

Most commercial mixed seeds are inclined to be short in sunflower seeds, it is advisable to get an extra box of the latter to put in with the mixed seeds. Also put out plain sunflower seeds for such birds as grosbeaks, chickadees, etc., I am personally opposed to feeding straight peanut butter, there have been incidents of birds choking on it. Be sure to supply fresh water, summer as well as winter. A bird bath should be placed near shrubs or small trees so that the birds can reconnoiter first before flying down to drink and bathe. A bird bath alone in the open is not practical as a rule.

If one is interested in nesting boxes, it is best to put them up in the fall so that they are established and have lost some of their newness by spring when the tenants arrive. There are specific birds which nest in boxes and shelters, and there are numerous publications that can be obtained for making these houses. A good one is "Home for Birds" U. S. Department of Interior, Fish and Wild Life Service Conservation Bulletin No. 14, U. S. Government Printing Office, Washington 25, D. C.

I have not mentioned any specific birds in this short article as the varieties in Maine besides the song birds, shore birds, etc., are too long a list to enumerate. But I do hope that with what I have written some stimulation of interest in this most absorbing study will result.

Additional References:

Enjoying Maine Birds, Maine Audubon Society, 22 Elm Street, Portland, Me.

Audubon Land Bird Guide, Richard H. Pough, Doubleday and Co., Inc., New York, 1949. This pocket-size book and its companion volume, *Audubon Water Bird Guide*, are of great assistance to the birder since they contain not only identification, but habits, voice, nest, and range.

Birds of America, Garden City Publishing Co., Inc., Editor-in-Chief T. Gilbert Pearson, President National Association of Audubon Societies.

Birds, A Guide to the Most Familiar American Birds, a Golden Nature Book.

The Laboratory of Ornithology, Cornell University, 33 Sapsucker Woods Road, Ithaca, New York, has records of songs and slides of the songsters. Supporting members receive their publications *The Living Bird* and the *Newsletter*.

Life Histories of North American Shore Birds, Arthur Cleveland Bent, in two parts, Dover Publications, Inc., New York, 1962.

Where to Find Birds in Maine

Olin Sewall Pettingill, Jr.
Cornell University Laboratory of Ornithology,
Ithaca, N. Y.

EXTENSIVE seacoasts, mountains, lakes, and coniferous forests are the natural areas of Maine most attractive for bird finding.

From Kittery Point, in the extreme south, to Cape Elizabeth near Portland, and northeastward to the mouth of the Kennebec River, the sea coast is low-lying with salt marshes, sand dunes, and beaches. Elsewhere, the shores are walled with rocks, ledges, and cliffs.

The mountains, mostly foothills, extend from the western boundary to the north-central interior where Katahdin, the highest in the state, rises seemingly alone. The lakes, over 2,000 in number, are fairly evenly distributed. Fresh-water bogs and marshes are numerous.

In the farmlands that occupy much of southern and eastern Maine nest birds of the fields, meadows, brushy lands, dooryards, and orchards:

Marsh Hawk	Brown Thrasher	Bobolink
Killdeer	Cedar Waxwing	Eastern Meadowlark
Eastern Kingbird	Robin	Common Grackle
Eastern Phoebe	Eastern Bluebird	American Goldfinch
Tree Swallow	Yellow Warbler	Savannah Sparrow
Barn Swallow	Chestnut-sided Warbler	Chipping Sparrow
Catbird	Yellowthroat	Song Sparrow

Where the farmlands have reverted to secondary deciduous woods:

Red-shouldered Hawk	Yellow-shafted Flicker	White-breasted Nuthatch
Broad-winged Hawk	Hairy Woodpecker	Red-eyed Vireo
Ruffed Grouse	Downy Woodpecker	American Redstart
Black-billed Cuckoo	Least Flycatcher	Baltimore Oriole
Barred Owl	Eastern Wood Pewee	Scarlet Tanager
Whip-poor-will	Blue Jay	Rose-breasted Grosbeak
	Black-capped Chickadee	

In the uninhabited northwestern sections, on the higher mountains, and along the coast east of Penobscot Bay, are forests of spruce, fir, and hemlock, mixed in the warmer areas with white pine, sugar maple, birch, and beech. From late May through early July, 15 or more species of warblers breed in these northern forests. Other birds include:

Goshawk	Olive-sided Flycatcher	Golden-crowned Kinglet
Spruce Grouse	Gray Jay	Solitary Vireo
Great Horned Owl	Boreal Chickadee	Purple Finch
Yellow-bellied Sapsucker	Red-breasted Nuthatch	Pine Siskin
Black-backed Three-toed	Brown Creeper	White-winged Crossbill
Woodpecker	Winter Wren	Slate-colored Junco
Yellow-bellied Flycatcher	Hermit Thrush	White-throated Sparrow
	Swainson's Thrush	

On the coastal islands between May 15 and July 15, nest impressive numbers of seabirds — Leach's Petrels, Double-crested Cormorants, Common Eiders, Great Black-backed Gulls, Herring Gulls, Common Terns, Arctic Terns, and Black Guillemots. A few Common Puffins nest on Matinicus Rock.

Reprinted from *Enjoying Maine Birds*, published by the Maine Auduborn Society, 22 Elm St., Portland, Maine.

Planting for Birds

Robert W. Patterson and Albert L. Prosser
Maine Audubon Society, Portland, Maine

WATCHING a Maine feeding station in January, you might get the idea that chickadees and nuthatches want nothing from life but suet and doughnuts; but in June the same feeder and the same free lunch will be poorly patronized. Birds still like natural foods when they can find them, and they find them where plants are growing. They must also have nesting sites, shelter from elements, and protection from their predators. Trees, shrubs, and groundcovers provide all these, and since different birds have different requirements, more species will usually be found where there is a variety in the size and type of vegetation.

Most of us confine our plantings to the grounds around our homes, and fortunately we can plant to please both the birds and our own eyes. For years, one of the best small bird-watching spots on the Maine coast was a large garden, planted with types of vegetation from herbaceous plants to small trees. What made this place unique to birds was not just the great variety of plants, but the meticulous care given to both plants and soil. All garden waste was composted, no weed-killers, almost no fertilizers, and a minimum of insecticides were used. Watering was constant in dry weather. Conditions were made perfect for the production of life — not only vegetable life, but the myriad of small animal forms on which so many birds depend. Birds stopped there in the spring, many nested, and hundreds came again in the late summer and fall. This garden pointed up two facts: (1) The kind of plant is less important than the right combination of trees, shrubs, and open places. (2) The better conditions are for plants, the better they will be for birds.

Most plants bear fruit of some sort, and most fruits are eaten by one or more species of birds; but it should be remembered that fruiting seasons are short, and that plantings should be designed to appeal to birds on a twelve-month basis. If a plant can provide bird food for a brief period (a shrub is sometimes eaten clean in a single day) and still fit into the bird picture for the remaining months of the year, well and good; but fruit need not always be the first consideration. In addition to size and character, a first consideration for most people in Maine is hardiness, since few want to give their plants winter protection. Coastal and southwestern Maine are in the same winter temperature zone as southern New Hampshire and northwestern Massachusetts, but northern Maine is in a class with southern Labrador and Quebec, Minnesota, and the Dakotas. Borderline plants may live here for years, only to die when an old-fashioned winter comes along. Maine planters should study plant lists with hardiness in mind.

The following brief list gives a few examples of plants of varying size and growth characteristics that are hardy in all parts of Maine, grow in average soil, and bear fruits that are eaten by a variety of birds.

Name	*Height in Feet*
TREES	
Siberian Crab Apple (*Malus baccata*)	50
European Mountain Ash (*Sorbus aucuparia*)	45
Bechtel's Crab Apple (*Malus ioensis*)	30
Fleshy Hawthorn (*Crataegus succulenta*)	15
SHRUBS	
Nannyberry (*Viburnum Lentago*)	30
Amur Honeysuckle (*Lonicera Maacki*)	15
Arrow-wood (*Viburnum dentatum*)	15
Highbush Cranberry (*Viburnum trilobum, v. americanum*)	12
American Elder (*Sambucas canadensis*)	12
Highbush Blueberry (*Vaccinium corymbosum*)	10
Winterberry (*Ilex verticillata*)	9
Tatarian Honeysuckle (*Lonicera tatarica*)	9
Bayberry (*Myrica pennsylvanica*)	8
Red Osier Dogwood (*Cornus stolonifera*)	7
Inkberry (*Ilex glabra*)	6
Witherod (*Viburnum cassinoides*)	6
Coralberry (*Symphoricarpos orbiculatus*)	3–6
Fragrant Sumac (*Rhus aromatica*)	3
Dryland Blueberry (*Vaccinium pallidum*)	3

Reprinted from *Enjoying Maine Birds*, published by the Maine Audubon Society, 22 Elm St., Portland, Maine.

Feeding Birds in Summer

Barbara Cheney

FEEDING birds in winter is an almost universal practice in the country, but people who winter in cities and do not love pigeons may find a summer feeding station rewarding. There is ample justification for such a program. It seems a pity to abandon the birds just as the busy nesting season begins. Anyone who has watched frantic parents trying to feed four or five squawking offspring will agree. No one should undertake this sort of catering business blindly. There is a fact which must be faced. In addition to the desirable visitors one will be forced to entertain starlings, grackles, red-winged blackbirds, cowbirds and bluejays, all noisy omnivorous eaters.

One may compromise. A homemade feeder can be built, rather like a birdcage on a pole. It consists of a platform with a hinged roof about 18 inches above it, a feeder within, the whole surrounded by fence or chicken wire, the holes large enough to admit small birds only. I have seen another device, a lobster trap placed on a broad flat rock near the ocean. Small birds can enter this easily. Both these compromises exclude, besides the obnoxious birds, many desirable ones who cannot enter. My method is to feed all who come. I buy sunflower seeds in 50-pound bags and store them in galvanized pails in the garage. At the height of the season my visitors consume 25 pounds a week. The husks have to be raked up and disposed of frequently. Mixed wild bird seed disappears much more slowly. Suet is impractical in warm weather. I have one high open feeder equipped with a most essential squirrel baffler. And I spread seed on a flat rock, for many pleasant birds are ground feeders.

My chipmunks are so well supplied with sunflower seeds that they never harm the garden. I also scatter bread crumbs on the lawn until the young birds are full grown. A bird bath is, of course, important. It should be placed in an open area with no near concealment for cats, and also where it can be refilled easily and often. Berry-bearing wild bushes are useful: honeysuckle, blueberry, cherry, blackberry, etc., and there should be down-bearing thistles to attract goldfinches.

All summer we entertain, besides the undesirables, purple finches, goldfinches, towhees, brown thrashers, song sparrows, rose-breasted grosbeaks, and mourning doves. Cardinals are in the neighborhood but do not venture so near the sea. Nuthatches and chickadees come early in the season and again later. Catbirds and robins, though not seed eaters, enjoy the bath and the bread crumbs. Hummingbirds like the flower garden. Gulls sometimes drop in to investigate the bread crumbs but we do not encourage them. Birds are untidy so the sanctuary should not be too near the house, neither should it be too far away. To sit in a comfortable chair, binoculars and bird book close by, and to observe these guests is a far more pleasant way of bird watching than to scramble about in wild country amid brambles, poison ivy and insects.

Tree Farms

Sarah R. Childs

OUR farm is a member of the American Tree Farm system and we, very proudly, display the green and white diamond-shaped sign at the entrance to our driveway. However, there seem to be a great many misconceptions as to what a Tree Farm really is. People come in wanting to cut their own Christmas tree, others would like to "pick up" a few trees inexpensively. A friend said, "You are a Tree Farm. What should I plant at the seashore in Virginia?" We don't grow Christmas trees, we don't sell trees, inexpensively or expensively, and, if I know what would thrive on the Virginia seacoast, it is not necessarily because we are a member of the American Tree Farm system.

A Tree Farm is privately owned, tax-paying forest land that is being managed for the most effective harvesting and continuing growth of forest crops. The size of the tract is immaterial.

The American Tree Farm system is sponsored nationally by the American Forest Products Industries, Inc. The purpose of the program is clearly expressed in the "Tree Farm Manual" of the Delaware Tree Farm Committee:

> "The American Tree Farm program gives public recognition to those private timberland owners who are doing outstanding jobs in the management of their forest lands, thereby encouraging others to do likewise. The basic aim of the American Tree Farm system is to place more woodland under management practices. That will bring continuing benefits to the owner and produce more and better forest products and services for the American people."

Properly managed wood lots also contribute a great deal toward the conservation of our natural resources and of our wildlife and, in no way, interfere with hunting, fishing or recreation.

You do not become an accredited member of the Tree Farm system just by planning to manage your wood lot properly in the future. Before you can qualify, your timberland has to pass a rigid inspection and you have to answer satisfactorily a great many questions on your past management practices.

Forest protection against fire, insects, and destructive grazing is of major importance. Roads through the woods are essential in case of fire, as is the proper disposal of slash. Diseased trees must be removed, and no grazing that would result in the destruction of seedlings is allowed.

Instead of clear cutting, which means the cutting off of *all* the trees in a given tract of land, selective cutting is a requirement. This means, literally, selecting only the larger mature trees to be sold for lumber, thereby giving the smaller ones a chance to grow. This results in more available lumber and more profit for the land owner.

If, after a cutting, or actually, at any time, there are not an adequate number of seedlings coming up naturally, it is necessary to plant small trees, which can be obtained for a few cents apiece.

Any private taxpaying timberland owner is eligible to have his land or a portion of his land certified as a Tree Farm provided he has been following these practices. All forestry personnel are asked to use their initiative in recommending for inspection any land that they think would qualify.

Once having passed all tests and inspections and having agreed to further periodic inspections, you are formally presented with your certificate and Tree Farm sign. We are very proud of ours, even if we do, occasionally, get odd requests from passers-by, as we feel that it is a visible proof that we are contributing to the conservation of our national resources and that it may, also, interest others in the program.

Two Ornamental Trees

Barbara Cheney

THE MOUNTAIN ASH is one of the most satisfactory trees to grow in this area. It is hardy, doing well in any sunny situation, even at sea level despite its name. The delicate foliage is attractive. In spring it has lacy white blossoms and in late summer is covered with spectacular clusters of orange-red berries, very popular with birds.

For exposed places near the ocean the NORWAY SPRUCE is unsurpassed. A very hardy evergreen, it is not troubled by salt spray or hurricanes. This spruce should never be used for foundation planting or placed too near the house for, given time, it grows extremely tall.

REFERENCES FOR ADDITIONAL INFORMATION ON
HARDY ORNAMENTAL TREES

Conifers of Maine, Native and Commonly Introduced, Fay Hyland, Bulletin 345 (Revised), Cooperative Extension Service, University of Maine, Orono, Maine

The Woody Plants of Maine, Fay Hyland and Ferdinand H. Steinmetz, University Press, Orono, Maine

Manual of Cultivated Trees and Shrubs, Alfred Rehder, Macmillan, New York, 1940

America's Garden Book, James and Louise Bush-Brown, Charles Scribner's Sons, New York, 1958

A History of Portsmouth's Street Trees

Constance T. Johnson

THE death-knell of the tree-surgeon's power saw has long echoed throughout York. At last Dutch Elm Disease claimed one of our own trees. The poignantly sad experience of watching it being felled brought to my mind thoughts of all the generations of trees which once grew in this seacoast area. They witnessed much of the growth of this country, and eventually their fate was, perhaps, not dissimilar to that of the elms of this day.

In old Chronicles about the environs of the Piscataqua River I had read accounts of the landscaping problems of our 18th and 19th Century conservationists. It might be of interest to recount one or two of these stories, since we are sometimes apt to wonder if horticulture was not more carefree in a bygone era.

One account, written over a century ago, speaks with regret of giant elms, then over a hundred years old, which were falling prematurely. Their huge trunks had been trimmed extensively to afford space for sidewalks which the public desired for Portsmouth, thus forgetting the harmful effect on the trees.

Many other elms, planted along Congress Street from the old Market, were lost in the Great Fire of 1813.

A systematic effort was made to beautify the streets of Portsmouth with ornamental shade trees, commencing about twenty years after the Revolution. Governor John Langdon originated the short-lived trend for planting Lombardy Poplars (*Populus nigra var. Italica*) in the area. The first trees were placed in front of his Mansion in 1793. The local gentry were so enthralled with the lush, thriving trees that they planted them on their own property and along most of the public streets, as well. Soon they lined what are now known as State, Court, Pleasant, and many other streets. These trees were carefully put out, and well boxed, having been sent, at a goodly price, from Boston. Unfortunately, within a score of years their beauty lessened. Their tops were broken by lightning and frost. New, unpruned, shoots grew out at random, and the poplars, now in disfavor, were found only in cemeteries.

These trees were gradually replaced by sycamores (*Platanus occidentalis*). Again, for a few years, these lovely green shade trees graced many a street. Our forebears were to encounter more difficulties, however. Scarcely twenty years passed before the sycamores became infested with caterpillars which made a network of foliage, to say nothing of dropping on the shoulders of passers-by. There was no community spraying in those days (would Rachel Carson approve?) so they soon had to be destroyed.

In time public-minded citizens promoted organization of the Portsmouth Tree Society. During the second quarter of the 19th Century there was widespread planting of elms and maples. A few of these venerable trees are still with us. Many elms, regrettably, are fast disappearing, succumbing to the immigrant virus and the need for wider streets. After over one hundred and fifty-odd years of watching the parade of history they, too, have become expendable.

My Spring Wild Flower Garden

Rosamond Thaxter

"WILD FLOWERS for my garden?" No thank you, I really do not need any. My wild flower garden is much too large and already well seeded. Let me name over the vanguard of the first Spring blooms before the army becomes too vast to enumerate. Even while the snow lies piled high and snowshoes are a means of country travel; in the swampy places pussy willows begin to burst their smooth brown jackets and shine in silver fur tufts, to give warning of what are coming.

Then with the warm days of April, under the leaves, like a nest of little gray kittens all furry and soft come the Hepatica. The buds straighten out into dainty blossoms, ranging in color all the way from a deep almost violet through the pinks to a pure white; just a few inches above the ground, with smooth liver-shaped leaves, which account for their unattractive name. Wrapping its compound leaf around it like a shawl against the cold wind, the frail bloodroot looks like a patch of the winter snow, and marks where the Indians of old found war paint for their faces and dye for blankets. The next flower stands a little higher above a petticoat of green leaves, the anemones brighten woods and open fields. They, too, are all shades from a very deep pink in a shady spot to clear white where the sun is brightest.

Always hand in hand with the anemones are the dog-tooth violet, that smooth stem and mottled pointed leaf suggest the trout for which the yellow lilylike flower is sometimes called. As I come from the oak wood all along the brook, a splash of gold, and the cowslip lift brilliant cups above shiny flat leaves. These make succulent "greens" for many a country household, who have long been enjoying digging dandelions. These by the way are a good old stand-by, and look very gay until the yellow heads and white fluff become too numerous on the front lawn.

But I am now crossing the fields, here are the little houstonia, their tiny blue eyes well suggesting their other name of bluets or quaker ladies. Nearby are the fluffy pussy toes, just like the pads on my kitten's feet, with stem and leaf so light they are almost white. As I stoop to examine them closer here is bright yellow cinquefoil and beside it the wild strawberry blossoms, giving promise of where to find the luscious fruit a little later. Then the violets, some people think of violets as being just a little purple flower, but oh, there are so many different kinds, large deep purple ones, some very light with the little veins delicately outlined, white ones growing in the swamps, and in my wood the yellow variety with the flower borne in quite a different way on the stem. When I see these I know that it is time for Preacher Jack to be calling all the people from his Pulpit. Do you know the three large leaves that form a canopy, and the thick spotted stem looking for all the world like a horrible snake?

As I turn to the pine woods through the fields, lavender geraniums wave their frail blooms, over lacelike leaves and in the rocky places columbine hang out their little jester caps red and yellow and full of honey. All around a gray granite ledge a mass of saxifrage stands with a tiny flower above a hairy stem, well worth examining.

Now in the pine woods in the silence which as a child always made me want to whisper, there are more and more treasures. Carpets of polygala or "bird on the wing" resembling in color the arethusa which may rarely be seen in the swamp. Standing straight and beautiful as any other orchid between its twin leaves are the pink lady-slippers, a joy wherever seen and the hiding place of the yellow ones, is a secret to be kept carefully. Gold-thread runs under the ground and pine needles with starry white flowers, white varieties of Solomon Seal, true and false, twin flowers, sometimes a white trillium and masses of partridgeberry and so-called Star of Bethlehem. Very rare in most places but plentiful in my swamp is the Buck-bean; this grows in the water, the stem eight or ten inches tall, and on it a white flower resembling a miniature horse chestnut blossom even to the touch of pink on the fluffy white, very fragrant. Blue flags remind one of the lilies of France. Perhaps if I am lucky I will find a pitcher plant setting a trap for unwary flies, who are attracted by the red flower and fall into the pitfall of the hollow leaves, from which none come out. The flies are caught by the pitcher plant just as I am, at the end of my story when I am trying to escape!

The Importance of Bees

Mrs. Arthur W. Ewell

IT is impossible in this short space to do justice to so vast a subject as Honey Bees. From the days of the ancient Egyptians, they have followed man wherever he has gone., and bees live around the globe. No other one insect has ever been found in so many different places and countries. In every age they have been making honey for our use, and were even used as warriors against the foe in mediaeval times (a practice the Germans are said to have followed against the British in Africa, in the first World War).

Maeterlinck, who studied their ways, and wrote his famous *Life* of them more than 50 years ago, refers to them as "these fierce insects," and as an amateur amongst them, in my own garden, that's about the way I would speak of them too. They are mysterious in their ways and wholly commendable in their efforts, and their usefulness is supreme, but I don't fine them "lovable."

In the Bulletin of the Garden Club of America for April 1946 there was printed a most charming map of a bee garden, filled with herbs and early Spring flowers, and the bees were to live in bee skeps, and to get plenty of food from the flowers at hand. But the bees have gone "modern," they no longer want a straw house to live in, and they wander far afield for their nourishment.

They use, now, a wooden "tenement" of two or three stories. The first floor, opening from a small platform in front, is the brood chamber or nursery, where the queen wanders around, laying eggs in the cells the workers make for them, and where she is waited on by her slaves. The upper stories are their storehouses for pollen and for honey. It's a good idea to place these hives with a windbreak behind them, and to paint each hive a different color, pale pink, yellow or blue. The bees' sight is very keen, but flying home with their load of pollen and nectar, it's a help to them to locate their own home by special flowers, shrubs, or color.

Woe betide the bee who makes a mistake, and tries to enter the wrong hive. Guards are out watching for such marauders, or for the robbers, who steal in to get food, and the intruder is promptly torn to pieces.

The hive holds one queen, hundreds of workers, and plenty of drones. The latter are the gay bachelors who literally do nothing. They are fed by the workers, but have no facility for gathering nectar or pollen, themselves. Their one effort is to fertilize the queen, and this they never do in the hive. The queen is mated in the air, and as she flies faster and faster up through the air in the blue sky, the quickest and strongest drone of the hundred following her, reaches her. The poor fellow loses his life in his effort, but the queen returns ready for her life work.

It is estimated a good queen will lay 3000 eggs a day in the cells prepared for her, and the workers give these cells the most meticulous care, and clean and feed the babies until they hatch out.

The great event of their lives is when the "spirit of the hive" moves them to swarm. No one has really fathomed the mystery of this great drama, but it will always take place on a sunny day. They leave their perfectly appointed home filled with pollen and honey, and take the queen with them; seeking a new strange place to live. As they cluster together, filling the air with their noisy buzzing, guards are out searching for a suitable place, and to tell the others where and when to start.

In my own garden, we are almost as excited as the bees. Everyone in the household comes out to view the swarm. A new hive is held in readiness, hoses and ladders are collected, and we watch to see just where the bees will alight. A great black, solid mass finally comes to rest on a branch, a trellis, or a stone wall. The bees will stay for some time awaiting the message where they are to go. Now we sprinkle them with water or smoke them, then try to shake the swarm gently into the new hive. If their queen is with them, they will probably stay, but if they don't like the new quarters, or are too high, or too far away to catch, they disappear into the blue and are lost. If there should be more than one queen in a hive, the battle royal is on. They fight and kill each other until one is left supreme, while the workers indulgently look on.

Bees are ordinarily too busy to molest you, but if they are frightened, with a cry of alarm, they summon help; others come at once, and sting you with fierce passion. They say there is only one way to cure a sting: "avoid getting one," and there is only one remedy for that: "run, run, run!"

Robert Louis Stevenson describes a walk where he heard the bees "bumming in the gardens" as he passed. A lovely contented sound, and such a good word for it; they do "bum" among my garden flowers, and each one carries home incessantly the pollen and nectar he finds. The bees push their bodies deep into the heart of a blossom to get both pollen and nectar. They brush against anthers and stamens, and get coated with pollen which brushes off on the stigmata of the next flower and thus fertilization follows. They work on only one type of plant at a time, and when that particular type of pollen is gone, will go to another variety of trees or plant. So, we choose the trees, shrubs and flowers they especially like for every season, and their help in fertilizing the flowers is what makes them so valuable.

We have noticed, ourselves, how much more fruit we have, since we had bees, and how full of blossoms the trees and shrubs become. In my garden, they love early crocus, early blossoming trees of every kind, Japanese cherries and dogwoods, and locusts, while they seem to leave severely alone, rhododendrons and laurel. In the bee garden plan I have already referred to, herbs have a large place, but except for sweet marjoram, sage, white clover and thyme, the herb has little to offer them. Hedges of rosemary and lavender on this map would be delightful for them and for us, but they would be hard to achieve in an eastern climate, and red clover and honeysuckle, they haven't long enough tongues to suck. All annual Summer flowers they like, but they must fly far afield and get from the wild flowers enough nectar to satisfy them.

In California, where they are most useful in the citrus trees, they will choose wild mustard if they can get it, and in our apple blossom season, they seek the lowly dandelion. In Maine, their choice is clover, wild raspberry, goldenrod and milkweed, and in Massachusetts fruit bloom, white clover, goldenrod and sumac. As the season wanes they must eat the less delicate wild flowers, and the trees have ceased blooming. Our linden trees are about the last to blossom, and the bees make the most of this opportunity.

In handling bees one must realize they have their favorites. It is claimed their master is their friend, and when, in olden times, he died, one knocked on the hive with the key of his house, to let the bees know he had passed away. Today they are very sensitive to sight and smell and one is warned to avoid lipstick and cocktails when approaching them.

I recommend bees most warmly in every garden and orchard, for their superb help in horticulture, and in honey and beeswax, but speak softly and tread warily, if you want them as friends.

A Gardener's Calendar

A Gardener's Calendar

JANUARY
The Armchair Month

Draw a plan of your garden.

Send for seed and nursery catalogues, and place orders early to avoid disappointments and substitutions.

Buy only from well recommended dealers — local nurseries when possible. Local stock will be acclimated and arrive in good condition.

Brush snow from evergreens before it freezes on — work with care so that no branches will be broken.

Use Christmas trees and greens for cover, especially over evergreen shrubs and plants that will burn in the winter sun. These may also be sprayed on a mild day with an anti-dessicant such as "Wilt-Pruf."

Watch cold frames carefully and ventilate with discretion. Water when necessary. Don't brush the snow off as it gives additional protection.

Save hardwood ashes for use in the garden later on.

Prune fruit trees on a day of January thaw.

Bulbs for forcing that have been buried outdoors or kept in a cool cellar or attic can be brought in successively.

⚬⚭⚬

FEBRUARY
Prepare to work

Prune grapevines on a day mild enough so that the bark and canes are pliable.

Watch perennials for heaving and firm back into place.

Continue to ventilate cold frame — avoid sweeping wind and be sure to close it early in the day.

Check tools and equipment and repair and replace where necessary.

Paint garden furniture. Handles of tools painted a vivid color will be easier to find.

Send out lawn mowers to be sharpened and avoid the later rush.

If water collects around plants during thaws, try to make a ditch so that it will run off.

Check covering on plants to be sure it is in place but not packed down too tightly.

Cut branches of pussy willows and other spring-flowering shrubs and trees to force.

Snowdrops, crocus and other small bulbs planted against the south wall of the house will usually bloom by Washington's birthday.

MARCH
The month of mud

Look for signs of spring! Geese about the 15th, robins, song sparrows, meadowlarks and peepers around the 21st. Pussy willows in pussy, and twigs coloring as the sap rises.

Do all possible chores now to avoid rush later.

Do not hurry, because of a mild spell, to take off winter protection — just loosen it.

Dormant spray may be put on trees, but delay it as long as possible so that more bugs are hatched out and so eliminated. Also, try to wait for the ground to dry out so that the lawn will not be cut to pieces by heavy spray equipment.

Complete spring pruning, cutting summer-flowering shrubs and evergreens for shape. Eliminate crossed and rubbing branches. Do *not* prune *spring-flowering* shrubs until they have finished blooming, or much bloom will be lost.

Weed and water cold frames. Grow the plants as cool as possible in preparation for transfer to the garden in late April.

Plant seed of annuals, tomatoes and peppers in flats in a sunny window on March 20th.

Seed lawns.

As soon as the ground thaws, plant shrubs and trees.

❧

APRIL
Now — WORK

Fertilize lawns.

Harden off plants in cold frames by leaving sash off except on freezing nights. Water as needed.

Follow approved fruit tree spray schedules with care. These are obtainable from the University of Maine, Orono, Maine, and the University of New Hampshire, Durham, New Hampshire, free of charge.

After the ground is thawed and dried out so that root growth can start, uncover the roses and the borders. Do this on a cloudy or rainy day.

Give roses a dormant spray.

Fertilize borders and roses with a heavy application of bone meal, and a light application of a good general fertilizer.

As soon as they are above ground, spray peonies and lilies with bordeaux mixture.

Separate summer and fall-blooming perennials as soon as soil is friable.

When the ground is ready (mid-April in New Hampshire and late April in Maine), sow seeds of hardy annuals such as calendulas, sweet peas, sweet alyssum, larkspur, poppies and many others. Sow carrots, beets, lettuce, and plant onion sets — don't plant tender vegetables or flowers yet.

Plant dormant rose bushes.

Move hardy plants from cold frame to garden the last week in April and fill frames with seedlings started in the house. These must be protected from both hot sun and cold nights. Keep the frames closed and shaded day and night for several days. Ventilate regularly and carefully until the newly transplanted seedlings are established. Then give as much air and light as possible.

Complete planting of perennials, shrubs and trees, except for Magnolias.

Plant pansies, English daisies, forget-me-nots and other spring-blooming plants as soon as they are obtainable.

Plant strawberry bed.

If slugs are present under mulch on borders or elsewhere, prevent damage to plants by sprinkling Snarol around them.

∽༄∾

MAY
It May be spring

From May first to tenth is the height of the land bird migration — particularly warblers, tanagers, orioles, etc.

Catch up on all the things you meant to do last month.

Brace yourself for the steady round of summer chores.

Keep a notebook of planting times, changes and improvements that should be made.

Harden off tender plants in cold frame, but do not plant them out until Memorial Day.

There is still time to plant evergreens.

Do not remove foliage from spring-flowering bulbs. Allow it to die down naturally as in doing so it forms and feeds next year's bulbs. Inter-plant with annuals to cover the unsightly foliage.

If desirable, tulips may be lifted as soon as they finish flowering. They may be heeled in somewhere to ripen, or treated as expendable and given or thrown away.

Stake peonies and delphinium before they get too tall. "Brenda-Braces" (available from Breck's), or peony hoops are best for this.

Plant dahlia tubers and gladiolus corms after the middle of the month.

Sow tender flower and vegetable seeds toward end of the month. Make successive sowings of vegetables from then on.

Pinch chrysanthemum plants when they are six inches tall.

Keep dead blossoms picked from pansies and other annuals.

143

Prune shrubs after flowering, and trim evergreens as desired.

Watch continually and spray or dust against pests and disease.

If a late frost threatens, cover tender plants with newspaper, or leave sprinkler on plants all night and until ice has entirely disappeared from them in the morning.

Plant dormant *and* potted roses.

Keep runners and blooms picked off of newly planted strawberry bed. Mulch it with pine needles.

❦

JUNE
Thirty Rare Days

Take time each day to *enjoy* the garden.

To keep plants growing without check: fertilize lightly, but often. Once a week if possible. Water *thoroughly* if the weather is decidedly dry. Keep spray program going.

Use cold frames for seeds of perennials, biennials, cuttings and chance seedlings. These can be better cared for in a frame.

Get the house plants out-of-doors.

Mulch.

Even the tenderest things may be planted out now.

Spray poison ivy with an eradicant.

Remove all spent blossoms from perennials, annuals and shrubs — especially from French hybrid lilacs, rhododendrons and mountain laurel.

Continue to pinch chrysanthemums and hardy asters to make them bushy.

Don't cut asparagus after July first.

Magnolia trees may be planted now.

Stake tomato plants.

Narcissus may be transplanted as soon as the foliage dies down, and while you still remember their location.

❦

JULY
One month of summer

It will probably be dry. Water thoroughly when really necessary instead of sprinkling frequently.

Divide and transplant iris and oriental poppies.

Continue to remove faded flowers to promote more blooms.

Stake early where necessary.

Keep cold frame watered and weeded, and shaded against intense heat.

Cut back delphinium to ground, feed and water. Protect new growth against slugs and earwigs with Snarol sprinkled around the plant.

Give chrysanthemums and asters a final pinch.

Fertilize roses heavily. Sweet peas and annuals may be fertilized lightly each week.

Prune wisteria to wanted size by pruning new shoots to eight inches. This will also promote more bloom for next year.

Go swimming.

❦

AUGUST

The month for Recreation

Contine with the program for July.

Give roses their last feeding August first. Continue fertilizing other plants, particularly peonies and annuals.

Cut back hollyhock and bleeding heart foliage to the ground.

Order bulbs that must be planted early: colchicums, sternbergias, narcissus and madonna lilies.

Remove old canes of raspberries as soon as they finish bearing.

Evergreens may be transplated as soon as the new growth has stiffened. Water thoroughly and keep watered.

Plant spinach and lettuce for use this fall.

Cut back annuals, fertilize and water well. If a few at a time are cut back, the garden will not look too bare.

Small plants from the cold frame may be planted in the garden.

Pull onions. Dry in full sun until tops are brown, then clean and store in a cool, airy place.

Watch for the shore-bird migration which begins in mid-August. Biddeford Pool, Maine, is a good place to see them.

❦

SEPTEMBER

Hurricane and Harvest

Consider critically the work of the season.

Bring garden notebook up to date with record of successes and failures, and suggestions for improvements.

Check markers and labels to be sure that they are in place and legible.

Consider installing the ever-useful cold frame.

Herbaceous borders can be remade at this time, as all but the fall-blooming perennials can be transplanted and divided now.

Plant new peonies and move old ones (only if necessary) on September 9th.

Plant all bulbs except tulips. Try colchicum and autumn crocus.

The month to plant evergreens. Soak well and keep soaked.

September is the best month in the year to sow new lawns.

Root-prune wisteria if it did not bloom.

Chrysanthemums may be transplanted, or bought, in full bloom and used as fillers in the borders.

Tie up long canes of climbing roses to keep them from whipping and breaking in the wind.

After the first frost lift and store dahlias, gladiolus, tuberous begonias and other tender bulbs.

Spray house-plants and move indoors before frost, and before the heat is turned on.

Be *sure* to pick pears when only *tinged* with slight color. Store in a warm, dark place and check daily for ripeness.

Be careful when picking apples and pears not to bruise them or to pull off the stem — rot will start.

It is not recommended that roses and other deciduous shrubs be planted in the fall in this area.

Watch out for frosts early in September and cover tender plants, especially tomatoes, beans, cucumbers, squash, dahlias and tuberous begonias. Often after this early cold there will be a long growing season.

If your trees and garden are drenched with salt spray from a hurricane, wash off as soon as possible with fresh water from the hose. This will often save nearly all of them.

∽✺⌐

OCTOBER
The Brilliant Month of Sapphire and Flame

Take time to enjoy woods and shore, and "October's bright, blue weather."

From the middle of the month on, watch and listen for the geese that will be flying south during the day and in the night.

Burn any material showing signs of disease or insects. Add the rest to the compost pile.

Any major garden constructions such as terraces, rock gardens, paths, etc., can be undertaken now when there is more time than in the spring.

Lift clumps of chrysanthemums which have finished and plant closely together in the cold frame. Water thoroughly, mark, and mulch with pine needles or other material that will not pack.

Be sure to cut all peony foliage to the ground and burn. Dust over crown with bordeaux mixture to prevent botrytis.

Complete lifting of all tender bulbs, corms, and rhizomes.

When digging Peruvian Daffodils (Ismene), take special care to leave all possible roots and tops intact. Winter at a temperature above 60 degrees.

Plant tulips out of doors.

Pot hardy bulbs for forcing indoors.

Root vegetables can be left in the ground until a hard freeze is expected. Parsnips can remain until spring and will be sweeter then.

Be sure to harvest squash before hard frost. Store in a dry place between 40 and 60 degrees.

Tomatoes should be picked. The green ones will continue to ripen on a sunny window-sill.

If the weather is dry, thoroughly soak all trees and shrubs and keep them soaked.

∽∾∾

NOVEMBER

Indian Summer

Gather some wild cranberries for sauce for the Thanksgiving turkey.

Tulips can still be planted.

Scatter Snarol on beds and in cold frames to discourage slugs that collect under the winter covering and nip off tender shoots.

A trench can be dug for next year's sweet peas and filled with manure or compost.

Continue clean-up of garden.

Collect, clean and put away tools and stakes.

See that all poisonous sprays and dusts are correctly labelled and safely stored.

Clean the sprayers thoroughly.

Keep leaves raked off lawns. If allowed to mat, the grass under them will be killed.

Roses should be hilled up for the winter after the ground is frozen. Collect soil to use for this purpose, and cover to keep from freezing.

Cut back canes of tea roses and floribundas to two feet. Strip off all leaves before hilling.

Tie down any canes of climbers that will whip in the wind.

Do not make the mistake of applying winter mulch too early as it will attract mice. Have your material at hand and wait until the ground is frozen hard before applying — perhaps not before January.

Don't put away all of the out-door furniture — there will still be days when it will be pleasant to have a sandwich in the garden.

DECEMBER
Snow for Christmas

The easiest way to protect young trees from being girdled by rodents is to wrap them with aluminum foil from the ground up two feet. Secure with Twist'ems.

Newly planted trees should be staked or guyed to prevent their being loosened by winter storms. If using guy wires, thread them through pieces of old hose to protect the bark wherever they encircle a trunk or a branch.

Winter covering is essential to prevent damage to plants by keeping the soil frozen, and by protecting them from the winter sun. Do not put in place until there are three or four inches of frost in the ground. Evergreen boughs are ideal for this purpose, but many other materials such as salt hay, pine needles or dry leaves may be used as long as they do not mat.

Ventilate the cold frame at the lee end for an hour or so whenever the weather permits.

Corrective pruning of trees and late-blooming shrubs may be done until new growth starts in the spring.

Yews and other evergreens may also be pruned and the greens used for Christmas decorations, or for winter protection in the garden.

Observe conservation rules when gathering greens from the woods. Conservation lists are available from The New England Wildflower Preservation Society, Horticultural Hall, Boston, Mass.

Have bird feeders in place well stocked with food.

It is not too early to order seed and nursery catalogues, especially those from foreign countries.

Garden books and magazines make welcome gifts for gardening friends.

Merry Christmas

M. P. H. and S. R. C.